How to be a bad cook

The ultimate quick guide

GW00382010

WORDS by: Ruth Finnegan

CARTOONS by: José Sépi

R&F

HOW TO BE A BAD COOK

Copyright © Ruth Finnegan 2024

ISBN 978-1-7394328-2-9

All rights reserved.

No part of this publication may be reproduced,
stored in a retrieval system or transmitted in any form or
by any means, electronic, mechanical, without the prior
written permission of the publisher of this book

First Edition 2024

Callender Press I callenderpress.co.uk I Milton Keynes

United Kingdom

Design and production by John Hunt at mapperou.com

CONTENTS

GREEN LETTERING CORRESPOND TO ANTHROPOLOGICAL SECTIONS

R&F

Chapter 1: WHY COOK?

Well, why not? Humans always have, haven't they? Well, not at the very start - when they hadn't yet started to use fire and sustained themselves by hunting (men) and gathering (women) they must originally have eaten meat raw. And maybe not often either, for bringing down game would not have been easy, though when it came it would be a matter for celebration and feast. And so for perhaps millions of years...

Away back

But then humans, our ancestors, started discovering the benefits of fire. One day some enterprising or careless being, deliberately or just by accident, dropped a piece of meat into lightning ignited fire, and – roasted meat! Surely it must have caught on quickly and then spread through the world.

Cooked food: a decisive turn in human history? Some say so, and see the move away from raw food and the advent of cooking as the critical moment that we became human. No doubt an exaggeration but – perhaps they have a point: humans, after all, are the only animals who cook.

Cooking is

Cooking increases the digestibility of many foods which are inedible or poisonous when raw. For example, raw cereal grains are hard to digest, while kidney beans are toxic if not properly cooked. There is something almost magical about the change in molecular structure caused by the thermal denaturation of ingredients. So cooking unquestionably has a practical use. But is there more to it than that? It is surely not just heating potentially edible material. It has become a rich human art.

Both the process itself and the resultant products are among life's greatest pleasures and experiences.

The art of food preparation is in fact one of the most important parts of our culture. Eating together is a way to connect with others. It is also a road to affirming and maintaining our identities. I think of a Vietnamese boat refugee that I know who after four near-death days at sea, was rescued and brought to Britain when she was a young child; when grown up and professionally established, one of the first things she did was to set up a Vietnamese food takeaway. As another Vietnamese put it "Our dietary customs after 30 years of war and occupation are the only tangible signs that we still exist as a people". True. There is almost no celebration that does not involve cooking in some form, from birthdays to weddings, from religious events to age-sanctified traditional ceremonies.

Finally, cooked food marks love and caring between friends and family members. It shows that someone wants you around, and happy, so much that they take trouble for you, they want to share their table, their cooked food, with you.

COOKING FROM AWAY BACK

It seems that people first cooked food around 780,000 years ago, and changing certain material objects through exposing them to heat appears to be a uniquely human activity. As cooks we are carrying on that deep, historical, revolutionary, human-creating legacy, think of that. So be aware, as you hold the whisk or cut up potatoes, or whatever, that the human age-old heritage is in your hands, good-bad cook that you are, a cog in the great journey of human history. Without you and your cooking, and that of those like you, where would we creatures be? When you cook you are one of a long, talented, human line. Be proud.

THIS BOOK

This book is a personal take on how to be a BAD COOK. It's not for already-good cooks (keep away!), or would-be chefs, or those who adore cookery books. It's for bad cooks (like me) who may actually be quite good but don't want to be tied down by time-consuming pretentious detailed "recipes". We merely want to produce enjoyable nutritious hot food with no fuss.

In other words it's for those who may quite like cooking but DON'T like spending money on way-out ingredients, all the latest fancy equipment, art-y hats and courses, or, above all, spending time they be using for something productive, like dreaming or writing novels or looking out at the trees like those outside my window.

You probably already have a few glossy cookery books with pretty coloured pictures photographed by professionals at huge expense (yes, some people make a career of it). People enjoy choosing them for you; I even sometimes fall for buying them myself (actually, to be honest, I like looking at them and picking up an idea or two and imagining ... but as for following all those detailed steps to the inch: no! Well, hardly ever). I frankly don't have time to search out those complicated out-of-the-way ingredients (I just make do with the ones I already have in), and whisking for hours, and a host of separate (and to my mind often un-needed) stages, and half a pinch of this and five-eighths of a spoonful of that and four different sized saucepans and six bowls and the whole day gone.

Well, I repeat, this isn't for THAT kind of cook. There are plenty of good books for them, bless them. It's for busy level-headed you who rather enjoys cooking but hasn't much time and is not going to make a fetish of it. It's for the "ordinary good-bad cooks" like the ones that have carried us down the ages. Like me. Like you.

WHAT YOU WON'T GET OR FIND

Exact quantities and measures. Why?

Lots of cookbooks do go in for these of course and by all means look them up for guidance if and when you want. But for this book – well, for one thing I don't know how many you're cooking for so the recommended quantities may be wrong from the start (the "for four people" – a common, exact-sounding, claim in cookbooks – could actually cover an immense range depending on the people and the context, what they're like, what kind of day they've had or are expecting to have, how hungry they are...). Your ingredients and your quantities are also going to depend on such things as how many onions or sweet peppers you happen have in, whether you've just run out of milk, if someone loves fish pie but not with a cheese topping, or dislikes garlic or over-spicy dishes. So just choose ingredients and, within limits, quantities to fit what you need.

You probably already have a feel for the kind of amounts that more or less fit your circumstances; if not you'll surely build it up (in good bad cooking there's always plenty of trial and error, all the better if there's a bit of a giggle there too). Actually, good-bad cook that you are, that's probably more or less (this is very much a more-or-less book) what you do already. This book is just a handy guide with a few biased ideas from my own imperfect experience (yes, to repeat, it's a book about how not to be perfect).

So, to resume, with the exception of a few processes where proportions do matter, I'm not going to go in for precise measurements but rely on your good sense – after all you are the one who knows who will be eating your dishes. Just be sensible, as, like all "good-bad cooks", you doubtless are already

As well as (mostly) no precise measures, you won't find:

Long menus designed for chefs, or 3-hour, 10-stage, 20-ingredient demands.

Separate lists of ingredients:

Yes they can be useful. But to be honest I always find them a bit constricting, as if the only way you can make this kind of delicious dish is to use these precise ingredients. To make it easier to find the basics you need for a particular dish I've *italicised* the main ingredients (apart from those already obvious from the title) that I happen have used recently but there are almost always alternatives. After all you're a creative bad cook, are you not?

Precise detailed step-by-step instructions:

Actually I see my suggestions here less as "recipes", more as pleasant ways of dealing with food: "treatments".

Glamorous technicolour photographs (well maybe occasionally):

Cleverly arranged cooked dishes. Good-looking presentation is an important part of cooking, fair enough – but who needs pictures to prove it.

Lots of garlic:

Sorry, I just don't happen like it very much. But naturally you can add as much as you like to anything you like (bought ready grated is the simplest).

An index:

Yes an index can be handy, specially in a long book. But it's also so – uncreative. You lock down on what you already know about so don't go browsing around and hit on things that make you go "Oh, good idea", "Mm I haven't tried that" or "I wonder " – that's the only way to be a creative-bad cook. Anyway this is a short book, logically (my logic of course) arranged and there is a detailed **Contents List** at the end.

A comprehensive guide:

It doesn't cover un-cooked dishes (well, I suspect a couple of exceptions slipped in) and there's nothing about special things for Christmas or Easter, or invalids, or for eating outside.

It's just what I've found to be a useful basis for good-bad everyday cooking in the busy lives of today.

Important note: Allergies.
If cooking for others check before you start that they ***don't have any food allergies*** (specially for *nuts*).

Chapter 2: POTATOES, THE STUFF OF LIFE

Spuds! Irish!

I used to think potatoes were a stock example of an unhealthy, unnutricious and fattening food. *Wrong.*

Potatoes contribute to a healthy balanced diet. As well as carbohydrate (necessary for energy) potatoes are rich in vitamin C and potassium, and a virtually fat-free source of B vitamins, protein, and fibre. At the same time – and somewhat to my and perhaps your surprise – potatoes are strikingly less calorific, and thus less fattening, than equal amounts of pasta, bread or rice.

Not that any of all that was what brought me to potatoes: they were just a taken for granted part of my life from my childhood. I grew up in Ireland, some of the time in a remote non-electric non-plumbed cottage in Donegal, no shops or roads or close neighbours, just fields and bog and sheep. My mother cooked over an open fire. Like those around us we lived on potatoes and milk (we had a cow), with occasional butter and marmite and sometimes a bit of oatmeal.

The fields around us were full of potatoes. In the winter they were stored in long covered pits underground – very effective so long as the rats didn't get into them! They did once. I remember vividly – I was seven at the time – my mother coming in devastated, saying "The rats have got into the potatoes, so how" (horrified) "how will I feed the family?" I don't know how she battled the rats but she must have won because here I am.

So potatoes are central to my upbringing and those of many many others. It makes sense to start with them.

10

Potato history

Potatoes have an interesting history, beginning not, as with many foods, in Europe or Asia but in the New World. The first records come from the Peruvian Andes at around 6000 BC where communities of hunters from the South American continent started to cultivate wild potato plants (bless them – we owe them a lot!).

Following on from that as it developed over many many intervening centuries the Incas were growing them around 200 B C. The Spaniards noticed their qualities when they invaded Peru, then Wolter Raleigh introduced them to Europe. Easy to grow, they were enthusiastically adopted and rapidly increased in popularity. They became the staple crop in Ireland particularly, continuing even after the disastrous mid-nineteenth century potato blight there when millions perished or fled to America. The result is that in many parts of the work today potatoes are the most commonly eaten vegetable, expected at just about every main meal of the day.

There are many different kinds of potatoes, not just the "red" and "white" varieties of many of today's shops (the varieties could be a chapter in itself but that information is easily available elsewhere). Here I will just focus on the basic ways to cook and eat potatoes (the somewhat similar sweet potatoes and yams can be cooked in much the same ways). So …

Basic potato-cooking methods

I feel a little foolish going into this, as I'm sure you know it already. But even after many years of cooking I still find that pointers from others can help, so here you go (I know you'll just skip the things you don't need).

Boiled Potatoes

Peel and boil. Boil in salted water till they're tender but still firm, then drain. A couple of things worth noting:

1. *Some people like to use a pressure cooker. As it happens I was never any good with them so won't be mentioning them again (if you normally use them you'll know already how to adapt things to that method).*

2. *For "boiling", you can equally use steam; if that's your preference, great, you'll know how to do it so don't need separate instructions.*

- Cook whole or cut up, as you prefer (cut-up is quicker)
- Cook with or without their skins as you wish. Myself I like the traditional with-skins way, remembering too that some of the most nutritious part of the potato is just under the skin which you lose if you peel them.

Boiled potatoes are lovely served with a swirl of *butter*, coarse ground *black pepper*, and if available some *herb(s)*.

Roasted Potatoes

- Roast potatoes are the traditional accompaniment for a meat roast. They are also great roasted on their own or with other root vegetables.
- Peel and, either whole or, more commonly, cut into large-ish wedges, partly boil them, drain them, then return them to the saucepan and shake the pan vigorously.

This roughens them and means that fat clings to them when you put them to cook round the roast. They end up beautifully brown and crispy.

- New potatoes can also be gently roasted on their own in a bit of *butter* (no need for the shaking treatment).

Fried potatoes

By this I mean *shallow* not deep fried (deep fry if you like, of course, but it's more dangerous and less good for you), ideally in *extra-virgin olive oil.* You may prefer grilling which produces much the same results but so long as it's in a heavy, nonstick pan I myself prefer frying, as you have more control over what's going on.

- Works best if cut into smallish pieces and fried in oil or butter, with other vegetables, plus if you wish a dash of soy sauce or sprinkle of grated cheese, till well-browned and crispy.
- Chips – cut potato into thin fingers and fry. To be honest I don't think this is worth the effort, you can buy fresh or frozen ready-cut chips designed to be baked in the oven which is much healthier, less oily, and just as delicious.

Olive oil history

Nowadays we take olive oil for granted as an essential ingredient for cooking, but it might not have happened that way. Fortunately for us, the olive tree, as we know in from fossils, originated some 20 million years ago in what is now Italy. Equally fortunately for us, some bright soul realised how delicious the fruit was, and, no doubt over many centuries, people developed ways of pressing it to extract juice – the oil. At any rate by about 100,000 years ago, olives were being deliberately used by humans, and by 3,000 BC olive trees were being widely cultivated in Mediterranean areas such as Crete. Olive oil became a core, highly prized, ingredient in Middle Eastern cooking. It is now widely used and often preferred over other cooking oils, above all in the precious and highly health-bringing form of extra virgin olive oil.

Mashed potatoes

- Peel and boil until tender, then mash

- Can be fork-mashed roughly by each person on their own plate before eating with whatever flavourings are available: *butter* is still my favourite those childhood memories – but *marmite, cheese,* or *herbs* are also good: anything really. A meal in itself.

- Or mash while hot before serving (this is what is usually meant by "mashed potato") – smash with a fork, potato masher, or whisk, with generous butter and a bit of milk or cream (best to add these gradually so as not to overdo it) till creamy and more or less smooth but not a puree.

- Can be eaten on its own, but also good with a range of your favourite flavours (herbs, grated cheese, marmite, soy sauce …), also as a good-looking and convenient topping for many dishes.

Baked potatoes

- Choose large reasonably good looking potatoes, leave skin on, make a cut in each, smear with oil or butter and rub in salt (coarsely ground sea   salt is specially good)

- Bake in microwave (for a soft skin) for a few minutes (4–6 depending on size), or hot oven (for a crisp one) for about an hour till the inside is tender. You can save time by starting in the microwave then give the potatoes a crisp skin by finishing in a hot oven for a few minutes.

- Baked potatoes are good, skin and all, as an accompaniment or (more often) as a meal themselves.

- They can be eaten with a variety of toppings or fillings, e g butter, grated cheese, tinned tuna/ salmon/ pilchards, bacon, baked beans, smoked salmon with cream cheese … whatever.

- Exceptionally convenient, as once in the oven they don't need attention, also a help if you don't know when you'll be eating as they don't spoil if left in a hot oven.
- Great when people are very hungry or cold (have some spares).

Potato skins

Pieces of crisp skin stripped from baked potatoes make great starters on their own or with a dip.

Potatoes as a topping

- Potatoes in various forms make an easy and good-looking topping; bake uncovered in a moderate-hot till brown and crispy.
- Mashed, either on its own or with your choice of flavouring, or combined with oatflakes to a make pastry-like dough (roll or press together), cover pie with this and bake in moderate oven.
- Grated with cheese.
- Cut into thin pieces, with cream or butter.

Left overs have many uses so it's not a bad thing to over-cater.

SOME FAVOURITE POTATO DISHES

Everyone's potato pie

Cover halved hard-boiled eggs in thick cheese sauce, top with mashed potato, cook uncovered in moderate oven (about 30 minutes or till top is brown and crisp). Wonderfully simple comfort food and one of my absolute favourites.

Cheesy family pie

As above but cover the potato topping with grated cheese before cooking.

French potato pie

Arrange several layers of thin slices of potato alternating with sliced onions flavoured with rosemary, mace, or other herbs, just cover with milk, white wine or stock, cook in hot oven, uncovered or with a topping of your choice.

Minted new potatoes

Boil gently with liberal seasoning of fresh mint leaves. Serve with butter.If they're real new potatoes (not just small ones) this is one of the most delicious meals ever.

Colcannon

Fry creamy mashed potato with well chopped cooked cabbage till hot through; if it looks a bit dry add some milk or cream to moisten. This is a famous Irish dish, quick and easy and perfect for using leftovers, either on its own or as an accompaniment. It's also infinitely adaptable: you can substitute other greens like watercress, sorrel, nettles); add onions; combine with chopped bacon (fry crisp before adding the potato mixture to the pan); divided into rissoles; or topped with more butter or a soft poached egg.

Bubble and squeak

A variant of colcannon and with the same basic method, but can be cooked till golden brown using vegetables such as cooked brussel sprouts or carrots rather than greens and with cooked sausages or other meat as part of the mix.

This is a great quick-and-easy use of leftovers from a roast dinner (hence a traditional Monday meal).

OTHER POTATO TREATS

Potato bread

Roughly mash skinned cooked potatoes, mix to a stiff dough by adding *oats*, press or roll together to finger thickness or less if you prefer, fry gently each side, cut into wedges.

- A lovely hot breakfast either on their own or with bacon.
- Leftovers are great toasted the next day, hot buttered (lots of butter if you're me …).

Rissoles

Fry rounds of mashed *potato* with some pronounced *flavour/herbs/ spices* of your choice until brown and crispy.

Fish cakes

Sandwich slices of *tinned fish* such as salmon or tuna plus if wished other *vegetables* such tomato or sliced courgettes, between thick layers of *mashed potato*, fry or grill till lightly brown.

Potato nibbles

Slice potatoes very thin, brush with *oil*, bake for about ten minutes in hot oven till brown and very crisp

OTHER ROOT VEGETABLES AND MORE

Many other *root vegetables* can be treated in similar ways, for example turnips (as, being Irish, I call them, "swedes" to you) , parsnips, carrots, Jerusalem artichokes, just taking account of their sometimes different shape, size or texture. Here are some examples (don't stick just with them).

Caramelised carrots

Chop into thick rounds and cook in uncovered saucepan or hot oven for 30-45 minutes with butter, a little *sugar, black pepper,* and *lemon juice* (plus if wished herbs – or scatter over when cooked) till tender, brown and well caramelised. My husband's favourite, and he was great at cooking it.

Creamed Jerusalem artichokes

Boil in chunks till tender, then mash or beat till smooth. Add further flavouring if wished, e g ginger. A lovely accompaniment to almost any main course.

Also great using parsnip or turnip ("swede" to you ignorant English folks)

Special fry

Fry any combination of root or other vegetables in oil or butter till brown and tender. Add chunks of sweet red pepper, tomato and courgettes (or etc) and your choice of herbs, or chopped bacon. For a treat top with buttered breadcrumbs. Eat very hot, maybe straight out of the pan. love this easy healthy mix, good for leftovers or emergencies.

Cauliflower cheese

Pretend a cauliflower is really a root vegetable so cut in chunks, cover with cheese sauce – can be made from bits and pieces of left-over cheese, even better from a mix of different kinds – bake in a medium oven topped with grated cheese till brown. This is good for just about any vegetable (for example broccoli, leeks or a mix).

Hot beets

Boil beetroot whole, unskinned; when tender nick skin and slip off in gloved hands (much easier than trying to cut off with a knife or potato peeler). **Serve hot with white sauce, sour cream or Greek yoghurt.** *They'll* look spectacular.

Beetroot history
Beetroots were domesticated in the ancient Middle East, primarily for their greens, and were grown by the ancient Egyptians, Greeks, and Romans. By the Roman era, they were also cultivated for their roots.

Onions
Onions are the essential, versatile, start to many dishes, specially soups or casseroles, and can also be treated in many ways like potatoes. If you find them a pain to peel and cut up – streaming eyes! – boil them first, leave them in the water for a few moments then slip off the skins; or, easiest, buy dried onions or, better, sliced frozen onions.

Onions in white sauce

Boil onions whole or halves, then drain and serve covered in white sauce: a plain and delicious accompaniment for any main course. Also good with a cheese sauce or a potato topping

Oven onions

Onions are great baked in a hot oven just as they are (not cut, not trimmed, not peeled) for 40-60 minutes depending on size. You can peel at the table by hand if you're feeling informal or with scissors before hand; ither way they are tender and delicious.

Globe artichokes

All right globe artichokes aren't a root vegetable, I just wanted to sneak them in somewhere, they're so easy and special. Actually, believe it or not, they are a kind of thistle! Boil or steam whole, one per person, till a leaf will pull off easily (about 35 minutes). Eat at table by pulling off the leaves one by one, dipping them in *French dressing* or *melted butter,* and eating the soft fleshy end of the leaf, then, finally, the "choke" at the centre. Very special and a wonderful companionable start to a dinner.

Generally

Don't spend time washing fruit or vegetables that are going to be cooked unless you think they've been contaminated on the way or there's earth to remove either outside or, as with leeks, inside. In the same way you don't need to peel fruit or vegetables before cooking (even tomatoes *whatever* the formal recipes say). This isn't the end of potatoes because that ever useful root keeps coming.

STOP!

Chapter 3: OATS, A BASIC HUMAN FOOD

In the form of oatmeal, porridge oats, or, easiest and, readily buyable, oatflakes or, for a smoother result, rolled or instant oats, oats have long been the basis of a substantial proportion of cooked food for human consumption.

It is a food high in protein and healthy fats, nutrient-rich and associated with lower cholesterol and reduced risk of human heart disease. Unlike the more delicate wheat and barley, it has vigorous growth, is relatively intolerant to pests and diseases, and can be grown even in poor soil and the cool, wet weather conditions of western Europe. In Ireland where I grew up, "corn" is always understood to refer to oats; in England it's wheat, in America maize.

Overall oats is a product that is healthier, easier to store, less dusty, and not so likely to burn during cooking than the commonly used wheat flour.

In fact I have by now given up on wheat flour and think you should too – unless by any chance you want to make a very light sponge cake (which I don't). For everything else that fancy cooks use flour for, try oats: thickening soups and casseroles, making porridge and muesli, and producing wonderfully chewy nutritious biscuits, and an unending variety of tea cakes.

In the treatments below, "oats" can be interpreted as either oat flakes, rolled oats, instant oats, or a mix of these. They give slightly different results (you may wish to experiment to see which you like best), but they all work.

Is it beetr or blood

BAKING

Unlike other cooking treatments, more or less exact proportions are important in baking, so I sometimes include precise measures (you can multiply up or down of course to suit your own needs).

Irish soda bread

Thoroughly combine 1lb oats, I tsp baking powder, and a bit of salt to taste, then mix in buttermilk or soured milk (made by adding a teaspoonful of light vinegar or lemon juice to milk, leave till curds begin to form – about 10 minutes), enough to make a tough springy dough (about 150mil), knuckle it around once or twice (not for long), flatten slightly, then put in a rough mound on an oven tray. Sprinkle the top with some more oats, then cut down into the top about two-thirds way through across both ways – this makes a cross in the top of the loaf or, as tradition has it, a "faeries' way"; more prosaically it means it will bake evenly, also that it will later separate easily into 4 "farls" (quarters or farthings).

Bake in a hot oven for about 45-50 minutes. When ready it sounds slightly hollow when tapped. If it seems not quite done turn upside down, bake another 5 minutes.

For a crisp crust, cool in the air, for a softer crust (my preference) wrap in cloth to cool. Best eaten on the same day (butter and/or honey go wonderfully), also glorious fried or toasted next day or later. So – you now have your own home-baked bread. Easy too once you've done it a couple of times (just whatever you do, don't overdo the baking powder and mix it in extra well).

This is just the basis; there are an infinite number of things you can add to the mix before you put it in the oven, like:

* Raisins or other dried fruit

- Grated cheese
- Seeds or nuts eg cinnamon or (specially nice) walnuts
- Soft or melted butter
- Spices
- Honey

Scones

Same ingredients and method, just divide the dough into scone size pieces, 10-12 mins in oven. These can have same variations as for the full loaf: grated cheese is specially nice. If spread with butter / whipped cream and strawberry jam the scones are marvellous for a luscious afternoon tea. Also with or without butter they are perfect as a side accompaniment for soup.

OATS HISTORY

Early humans relied greatly on wild plants, including many kinds of grasses from which as early as 100,000 years ago they collected the seeds for food. Among these plants were various species of wild oats, native to Europe and Asia. Palaeolithic hunter gatherers were already hand grinding their grain for food 32,000 years ago.

The deliberate *cultivation* of edible grasses came later, however, starting, it seems, somewhere in Bronze Age Europe. The process spread – then, as now, and for both good and evil, humans were great imitators – and agriculture, including of oats, became established worldwide.

The Romans introduced oats cultivation to Britain in the first century BC where it flourished as a low maintenance crop well suited to the climate: it adapts better than other grains to cool and wet environments. Oats were particularly popular in Scotland.

Samuel Johnson's 1755 dictionary neatly defined oats as "a grain, which in England is generally given to horses, but in Scotland appears to support the people" (the riposte was "That's why England has good horses, and Scotland has the finest men!"). They were valued in England too where oat bread was first manufactured, its first factory being established in 1899. There were no native oats plants in the New World, but oats and other grains were brought to North America in 1602 and planted on the Elizabeth Islands off the coast of Massachusetts. By 1786 they were popular enough for George Washington to have sowed 580 acres of oats. By the 1860s and 1870s, the main cultivation of oats had moved westward into the middle and upper Mississippi Valley, its major area of production today.

Oats, an annual plant, are nowadays of major commercial importance, grown throughout the temperate zones of the world. They have a vigorous growth, are relatively free from diseases and pests, and have a lower heat requirement and higher tolerance of rain than other cereals, making them particularly suited to areas with cool wet summers such as Northern Europe.

Looking back, we can see that the development of agriculture, including the transformation of a weed – the wild oat species – into a cultivated plant millennia ago, was a momentous step in human history, independently developed in separate regions of the Old and New World about 12,000 years ago. It enabled the establishment of settled villages and the many cultural developments based on an agricultural rather than hunter-gatherer form of livelihood. In due course various mechanisms were also developed for ploughing fields for cultivation and for pounding and grinding the harvested grain: heavy tasks when, as at first, they were all done by hand.

By now oats in various processed forms is an easily obtainable and standard culinary ingredient. Though generally cultivated later than wheat or barley, oats have thus been grown, cooked, and eaten since early times, providing basic and nutritious foodstuff ever since – even the ancient Greeks, we are told, liked porridge!

So behind this common ingredient there is a long history – which but for human inventiveness over the millennia might, indeed, never have happened. It is satisfying for us cooks to remember this history as we reach today for our humble oats to transform them through our culinary art into bread, puddings or breakfast porridge.

OTHER OAT PRODUCTS

Oat pancakes

Mix a handful of oats with an *egg* and enough *milk* to make a thickish batter, and fry in a hot pan in small spoonfuls (about 10 to12 in a medium pan); extra nice fried in *butter*. Turn when brown and crispy and eat at once, preferably straight from the hot pan. Lovely as they are but I sometimes squeeze some lemon juice or the remains of my breakfast orange over them and/or sprinkle with crunchy caramelising sugar.
You can also vary by adding grated cheese or roughly chopped apple to the batter.

Banana pancakes

Another variation (not, this time with oats – sorry to cheat but they're worth knowing about): one banana (preferably really ripe, almost ready to throw away) mashed together with one egg, then roughly beaten to a batter (there'll still be some banana lumps, if it's me anyway, but that makes it taste all the nicer), NO FLOUR OR OATS. Fry in the same way as oat pancakes but they take a bit longer to firm up before ready to turn over.

You CAN do any of these pancakes as a single crepe covering the whole pan but it does tend to break up and look very untidy when you turn it over – it tastes just as good however, even better with a spoonful or two of raspberry jam smeared over it. *Pancakes are my favourite breakfast, but good any time of the day.*

Fritters

Make *oat* batter above, and dip rounds of *apple* or *banana* (or other *fruit*) into the batter before frying. Extra delicious if sprinkled with brown *sugar* and caramelised briefly in the pan before serving.

Toad in the hole

Bake *sausages* (any kind) in a very hot oven till cooked and smoking hot, pour the *oat batter* (made as above) over them and continue to bake at slightly lower temperature till the batter has risen and is light brown and crusty outside (25-30 minutes). *A meal in itself and always a favourite. Sausages are the traditional choice but other things are equally possible.*

Oatcakes

Mix oats, a dab of *butter*, *salt* to taste, and enough *water* (easiest if it's hot, and added gradually) to make it bind together into a ball as a dough that you can roll out (not too thin). Cut into rounds and bake in a medium hot oven until it is hard (about 25 minutes). *Oatcakes can be used as an accompaniment for soup, or, topped with pâté, cheese, smoked salmon etc, as a starter or snack.*

Topped toast

Fried or toasted *bread* is good with any kind of *topping* you enjoy, spread on after it's toasted. I specially like peanut butter (spread thickly), cheese (any kind, sliced or grated, or fried or grilled till brown and crispy), and avocado (scoop out avocado flesh, mash roughly with some lemon juice and a generous amount of seasoning, pile onto the toast).

Proper Yorkshire parkin

An age-old sticky chewy cake based on *oats* and *black treacle*, with a robust flavour that improves with time (it's best to use exact quantities) Beat I *egg* and 4 tablespoons of *milk* together. Melt 12oz *treacle, 3oz soft brown sugar* and *7oz butter* in a large pan until the sugar has dissolved, stir in 12oz oats, a tablespoon ground *ginger*, and a teaspoon of , spice then the beaten egg and milk. Pour into an oblong oven tin, top with sprinkled sugar, *seeds* or flaked *almonds*, and bake in a moderate hot oven until it feels firm and a little crusty on top (about 50-60 minutes). Cool in the tin, then wrap in foil and leave to mature for three days or more before eating.

This age-old recipe is associated with the month of November, specially with the first Sunday of the month known as "Parkin Sunday". In Yorkshire it is a traditional part of Bonfire Night Guy Fawkes Night), with the cake eaten as part of the festivities.

Biscuits

Chocolate buttons

Mix a handful of *oats*, a similar amount of *butter* or margarine, tablespoon each of *sugar* and of drinking *chocolate* or melted whole chocolate. Bake in teaspoonfuls, well apart (they spread), in a medium oven for 15-20 minutes or until light brown (not burnt!) and firm. A huge favourite in our household.

Oatey biscuits

Mix equal amounts of *oats* and *butter* or margarine with *sugar* to taste (a couple of tablespoonfuls). Roll out and cut into biscuit shapes, then bake in a medium low oven till firm and a little brown (about 40 minutes – watch out near the end, they burn easily).

They are lovely plain, but can be varied near–infinitely with various flavours added to the mix before baking such as honey, ginger or chocolate, or pasted in pairs with cream filling.

Leaping ginger biscuits

Same but use roughly chopped stem ginger and allow to spread out, untrimmed, in baking

Shortbread

Combine 6oz *oats*, 4oz *butter*, and 2oz *sugar*, roll out fairly thick, then either in one piece (to be cut into triangles after cooking) or divided into about 15 biscuits (making an attractive dot pattern on each) bake in a medium hot oven till firm but not brown (about 30 minutes).

BREAKFASTS

Porridge

Bring *oats* with two and a half times the amount of *water* or *milk* to boil, then stir, simmering, till smooth. Alternatively heat uncovered in a microwave till smooth (5-6 minutes), stirring once or twice.

Some like it with salt (add before cooking), others prefer sugar/syrup/honey on top when cooked, with added *milk* or *cream*. A traditional, warming, and nutritious start to the day.

Muesli

Mix a handful of *oats* with a variety of *fruit* (dried or fresh – *apple*, chopped, is very good), *nuts*, and/or *seeds*. Add *milk* or *cream* to serve and if wished brown crunchy *sugar*.

Some like to leave it in the fridge overnight, but assembling it next morning is fine too.

Generally

There are always plenty of variations on the basic recipes described here, so I guess you will follow your imagination to get the result you like. These are merely suggested treatments that have worked pleasantly for me, not follow-to-the-inch dogmatic recipes. Your variations are likely to be every bit as good as mine, quite likely better.

Another thought – this one is obvious, you maybe know it already but feel guilty about it: *don't* go to great trouble to do everything in innumerable separate stages and some special order as in the grander cookbooks. It's (almost) always all right just to sling things in, mix everything together (roughly, with a knife, is okay so long as any baking soda is well combined), so just – relax and enjoy it!

Chapter 4:
EGGS EGGS EGGS – THE SIMPLE THING

Eggs are the miracle ingredient. Hundreds of dishes depend on eggs, only a minute fraction of them included in cookbooks. Some years ago there was a theory around that eggs were too rich for you to eat more than once or twice a week; and, in parts of Africa, that they were not good for women and children. Fortunately that idea has gone by the way, and three or four a day (in my case sometimes more) is fine, and there are plenty of cooking methods to keep up the variety. Furthermore an egg, they say, carries the full nutritional value of a whole chicken. As a food, eggs are everywhere. This near-ubiquitous presence in human diets is actually scarcely surprising if you consider their history and antiquity.

EGGS HISTORY

As a human food, eggs have been around for a very very long time, six million years at least, and are among the oldest of human foodstuffs. In fact millions of years before humans developed agriculture, birds' eggs were a food. After all birds, descendants of the dinosaurs, had been on earth for millions of years before humans so their eggs had long been there for the taking. In the early days of human history when food depended on hunting and gathering, it is likely that women, the gatherers, took eggs from nests in the wild (well do I know the value of wild birds' eggs from having lived for a time in a small village in West Africa where food was scarce and where I was only too glad to eat the wild eggs there, however small). We don't know who first ate cooked eggs but what researchers tell us is that people living in Egypt and China were the first to keep hens. Long before that people must have found the virtues of eggs, whether raw or, in time, cooked, and the advantage of having a ready supply always close at hand. So there came, in time, domestication of the wild red junglefowl, the ancestors of our modern poultry. "Domestication"? Well that is how, from a human viewpoint, we naturally describe it. But perhaps, as with dogs, it was just as much, or more, the other way round: hens – we now know they are very intelligent creatures – made their nests near human habitations and adopted us, alert to the advantages of being near humans for warmth, shelter, protection from wild animals, company (hens like human company and, like dogs, can somehow be subliminally aware of when their owners are on their way home) and, doubtless most important of all, scatters of leftover food. So domestication became established as a symbiosis – a living together of humans and fowls to their mutual benefit.

Though we don't know how or where it first got going as an organised way of harvesting eggs we do know that people in Southeast Asia were collecting chicken eggs for food by 1500 BC (eggs of other birds, such as ducks and ostriches, were also eaten regularly but less). Boiled eggs were eaten in Ancient Egypt, while Romans liked scrambled eggs cooked with vegetables and spices; and baked egg custard was apparently invented by the Roman cookery expert Apicius in 25 BC.

Domestic fowl did not come to North America until 1493 when Christopher Columbus brought chickens with him on his second voyage – so the chickens that lay the eggs Americans eat today are almost certainly the descendants of those Columbus had on board. In relatively recent times egg production has evolved from a widespread backyard practice to the organised national and international industry of today. So humans have been eating eggs for millions of years. No wonder there are hundreds of ways of cooking them.

Basic egg dishes

Boiled eggs

Carefully lower eggs, in shells, into simmering water. For soft-yolk eggs, boil gently for about 4 minutes (more, or less, depending on the temperature and size of the egg(s). For hard boiled eggs, boil for about 8 minutes. Useful in salads, sandwiches, pies, also as a starter. To peel hard–boiled eggs: immediately plunge while still hot into plentiful cold water (stops a black line developing round the yolk), batter the shell gently all over to crack it, then slide the shell off (mostly this works a dream and is quick and easy, sometimes, I don't honestly know why, not).

(All right, you know all this already, lots of what follows too no doubt (well, after six million years ...). But maybe there'll be the odd thing you'll be glad to pick up ...)

Fried eggs

Crack carefully without breaking the yolk into a moderately hot oiled pan and fry gently until the transparent liquid round the yolk is white and firm but the yolk still runny. Some like it turned over but the commoner way, at least in Britain, is to serve it unturned: "sunny side up". Fried eggs are central to the traditional "full English breakfast", usually combined with *bacon, fried bread, tomatoes, mushrooms* and/or *baked beans* and sometimes yet other things.

Poached eggs

Drop de-shelled eggs one by one, unseparated, into a pan of simmering water, and simmer for about 4 minutes till the whites look firm and puffy, the yolks still soft. Alternatively use one of the specially designed poaching containers (one per egg) with the simmering water about two thirds the way up the container.

This is traditionally served on top of a piece of *toast* as a breakfast dish or a light lunch,

French toast

Make a batter by shelling and briskly beating one or more *eggs*, then dip in a piece of *bread* (alternatively leave the bread to soak up the batter overnight). Fry gently, preferably in *butter*, over a moderate heat until golden brown.

Lovely if sprinkled with *lemon juice* and *sugar* while still in the pan, thus becoming lightly caramelised, and/or topped with runny *honey or maple syrup.* Another version, specially (but not only) as a breakfast meal, is to accompany it with fried *bacon* and/or a *fruit* such as sliced orange or (especially good) banana.

Dipping something into an egg batter before frying is also good for food such as fish (in many countries the traditional dish on a Friday), scampi, chicken pieces, or bananas.

OTHER EGG DISHES

Colourful eggs

Fry sliced onions, *sweet peppers* cut in long strips, and garlic (if wished) in *extra virgin olive oil* over a medium heat, together with spices (eg cayenne pepper, cumin and caraway seeds etc), a spoonful of *tomato puree*, and a tin of *tomatoes* (with juice). Simmer uncovered till reduced to a good sauce – not runny or dry (about 10 minutes) and add some roughly chopped fresh *herbs* such as parsley and coriander. Break one egg per person into a cup and drop them carefully into small wells made in the sauce. Cover and cook until the whites are set and the yolks still runny (5-8 minutes). If wished sprinkle with cheese and serve with yoghurt on the side.

Eggy carrots

Cut carrots into long thin sticks, dip them into beaten egg, roll them in finely grated *parmesan* or other *cheese*, sprinkle with *salt* and *pepper,* and bake in a very hot oven for 15-20 minutes. Great on their own but also good for dips.

Marisol, a South American dish

Fry chopped onions, diced *ham and peas*. Stir this mixture into a large, deep, oven dish containing eight eggs, 3 tablespoons *olive oil, garlic powder, 1 pint milk* and *salt*. Cook uncovered in a moderate oven till golden, top with *mozzarella cheese*. Divide into portions and serve with tomatoes and/or a green salad.

Golden'd eggs

An unusual (Chinese) dish. Simmer eggs gently in their shells in water with *onion skins* for several hours, or overnight in low oven; when peeled they have a lovely yellow colour and flavour, good in salads or, with potato, as a main dish.

Eggs in cheese sauce

Cover halved boiled *eggs* with *cheese* sauce, top with a layer of mashed *potato,* cover with grated *cheese,* and bake in moderate oven till top is browned (about 30-40 minutes). The ultimate, easy, comfort dash, I love it.

Seeparated eggs

Meringues

Beat 2 *egg whites* till stiff and standing up in peaks, then gradually beat in 4 oz *caster sugar*. Bake in small spoonfuls set well apart on a baking sheet covered with oven paper (they tend to stick otherwise) in a very low oven till firm and light brown (about an hour and a quarter).

For attractive variations, add a little *coffee* or *chocolate powder* to the mixture before baking. Pairs sandwiched together with *whipped cream* make a lovely last-minute dessert.

Pavlova

Use the same meringue mix as above but spread out in one piece with a small weight in the centre before baking. When ready lift out carefully (it doesn't matter if it cracks or looks uneven), top with *fruit* and and a pile of *whipped cream*.

Chapter 5: SOUPS, EVERYONE'S SUPPORT

Soup is the greatest comfort food and easily made. It's hot, sustaining, and enjoyable, and can be made from almost whatever ingredients you happen to have in your cupboard.

It's convenient in lots of ways too, but it *can* take a bit of patience: slow and steady, simmering not hard boil, and not rushing to heat up fast (well except, as all good-bad cooks well know, when ABSOLUTELY NECESSARY). Unsurprisingly soup has a long history.

SOUP BEGINNINGS

The first bowl of soup was probably prepared around 20,000 BC. It is assumed that people began cooking soup as soon as they started making mud vessels or clay pots (you couldn't have soups or casseroles before that). There is some evidence that soups had become part of the regular menu in many civilisations from 6000 BC onwards. *Now too? Very much so.*

I'll focus here mainly on cream soups (thick) as these are the kind I like best: well, they *are* the best! (but to keep it fair there's a small bit about thin soups later). Just DON'T, as many people do, and as most recipe books tell you, use flour to thicken thick soups. Flour sticks and burns and anyway isn't anything like so good for you. Instead use *oats* or *red lentils* or *potato*, that great staple. That makes for a lovely thick nutritious consistency and with very little bother.

The base? Almost all good soups begin with heating chopped onions and potato, plus at any other *vegetables* you're using, *slowly* – 15 minutes or, better, more – in a little *butter* on a very low heat ("sweating" them). Then add *liquid:* water or milk or made from a stock cube or marmite or bovril or wine or a mix of these depending on the flavour you want to end up with, then and bring slowly(ish) to a simmer (don't boil hard).

Once the ingredients are tender continue to simmer gently to bring out the flavour. Then, when you're ready, liquidise for a smooth soup (the most popular); but leaving it a little chewy is good too.

From this base there are a multitude of differently tasting soups that you can make on top of the stove or in a slow cooker or, covered, in microwave or oven. They're very convenient as you can prepare them in advance then leave on a low heat till you're ready to eat.

Serve soup looking beautiful with interesting toppings (see below), either in separate bowls or in a large attractive tureen with ladle to match.

Here are a few of my favourites, starting from that same base – and no, to repeat, I'm not giving quantities, any bad–good cook knows these are adjustable to the people, settings, appetites, ages, tastes, seasons, what have you.

The liquid for cream soups can be stock, wine or, often best, milk.

MILK HISTORY

Human consumption of the milk of non-human animals dates back not to the very beginning of human history, but to the era when they started to domesticate animals during the Neolithic Revolution probably alongside the development of agriculture. This occurred independently in several places in the world from as early as 9000-7000 BC in Mesopotamia to 3500-3000 BC in the Americas.

Potato soup

Potato soup on its own is fine, in fact delicious, nice with just some *herb*(s) on top (I specially like mint and parsley myself, but basically any herb or spice you favour).

Nice variations are

- Potato and leek – a well-known soup and rightly so.
- Potato and (a lot of) parsnip.
- Carrot with ginger or (liquidised with the rest) cashew nuts.
  Lovely colour.

NUTS HISTORY

Nuts and fruits were probably, with seaweeds, the earliest foods consumed by humans, and have been a popular food even since – tens of thousands of years. A recent archeological dig in Israel found remnants of seven types of nuts and a variety of primitive nut-crackers that scientists believe date back 780,000 years. An excavation in Iraq uncovered evidence of nut consumption in 50,000 BC while in Texas pecan shells were unearthed near human artefacts that probably go back to 6,000 BC. There are many references to nuts in ancient times. One of the first recorded references is in the Bible: in their second journey to Egypt, Joseph's brothers brought almonds and pistachios to trade for grain.

And in the book of *Numbers*, Aaron's rod miraculously buds and bears almonds, proving he is God's chosen priest.

Almonds have in fact long played a significant role, both symbolic and material. They were a dietary mainstay of the people of the ancient Middle East, while the Romans made candied almonds, giving them as wedding presents as a symbol of fertility (a tradition continued to this day). In the Middle Ages, people ground almonds into flour, and many recipes used almond "milk" made from ground almonds. Almond oil was used as a medicine in many European and Middle Eastern cultures before the time of Christ and supporters of natural medicine still use it today for treating indigestion and other ailments.

Pistachio nuts also have a long history. In the Bible, Jacob's sons liked pistachios, and they were apparently among the Queen of Sheba's favourite foods. In legend, lovers who meet under a pistachio tree on a moonlit night will fare well if they hear the nuts crack.

Like so much else, pistachios probably originated in the Middle East. Traders brought them to Europe from Asia around the 1st century AD but they didn't reach America until the late 19th century.

Walnuts are another favoured food, still often gathered wild and with an age-old history. Ancient inscriptions indicate that walnut trees were grown in Babylon's famous Hanging Garden, and they were a regular part of the diet of ancient Greeks and Romans. Walnuts come into Greek myth too, as the god Dionysus turned his love into a walnut tree when she died. Romans considered walnuts food for the gods, walnut oil was used extensively in the Middle Ages, and peasants ground up walnut shells to make bread.

Walnuts arrived in the Americas with Spanish priests in the 18th century.

The first settlers in America learned about pecans from Native Americans with the result that Spanish colonists in northern Mexico were cultivating pecans in the early18th century. The first pecan tree planting in North America took place on Long Island, New York, in 1772 from where pecan cultivation spread south to Mexico, and the nut became an important commodity. In fact, founding fathers George Washington and Thomas Jefferson are both known to have grown pecan trees. Pecans were so valuable in the early 19th century that in some areas growing pecans became more profitable than cotton.

It is easy to see why nuts have been so popular through the ages. You don't have to track and kill a nut. In fact, nuts were one of the first convenience foods; not only can they be easily carried, they can be stored for months, making them great for long hard winters. Nuts are also rich in fat and protein, which make them filling and nourishing. You can eat them straight out of their shells, press them for oil, mash them for nut butter, cook with them. Nuts are also important because of their nutritional properties and have also been used in the past by various peoples as drugs to prevent or treat diseases

So nuts were, understandably, crucially important to early humans, as to other primates, at the stage when they were mainly gatherers, not yet even with the tools – weapons – to be hunters.

We would be wrong however to think of food gathering as just something of the distant past, no longer of interest now. Some people are still partially or even perhaps mainly dependent on gathering today. In recent times I think of my own family during the *Second World War living in our small cottage in Donegal, my father away for his work, my mother with her three children – myself, seven, and my two young brothers. With our help – children can indeed help in gathering and we loved it – my mother fed us not just on potatoes and, when she could get them, eggs, but through products from her gathering activities: nettles made into soup, wood* sorrel and dandelion leaves for salad, blackberries, beechnuts, crab apples, wild strawberries and raspberries. Then at certain times of the year there were wild, hazelnuts, sweet and soft in the early stages, later with shells to be cracked. There shellfish (not for nothing was our bay known as "The cockle strand"), rock crabs (terrifying to us children), seaweeds, and huge edible mushrooms that came in profusion once a year. My mother would like to to have progressed to cultivating as well, but the multitude of wild rabbits forbade (they revelled in her planting, all those lovely green shoots conveniently laid out for them!).

As for other gatherers or partial gatherers, past or present, we had a good diet.

Beetroot soup

Made, like the other soups here, from the base above but with beetroot being the predominant ingredient, this has a superlative distinctive taste and (if re careful not to boil it too hard or long) a wonderful rich red colour. Either hot or cold (the famous Russian *bortsch*) it looks spectacular specially if you serve it with some swirls of *cream* over the top.

Jerusalem artichoke soup

This, prepared, if you prefer, with a little *lemon juice* and preferably very smooth and thick, has a unique and wonderful favour.

Celery and/or celeriac soup

With a very unusual taste this, made extra thick, is good either on its own or with *fennel*.

Pea and mint soup

Exceptionally quick and easy, as if you are in a rush you can omit the usual base and just use a pack of minted frozen peas. Cook quickly in water or *milk*, liquidise and it's perfect for emergencies. Swirls of *cream* on top make it look wonderful and show what a caring and "good" cook you truly are.

Pumpkin soup

One of my favourites, made from peeled and cut up pumpkin, *onion,* and *ginger*, liquidised to be very very smooth. It can be served either hot or, in a tropical climate (I first cooked it in Fiji), chilled.

Nettle soup

All my mother's soups were great – this was where I learned that you didn't need to be a "good" cook to be marvellous – but nettle soup was her super show piece (the spinach version is good too, just less romantic). Starting from the usual base, heat the leaves in water, milk or stock, liquidise and serve. Be sure to boast (specially if it's true) that it's from wild *nettles* and that you gathered them yourself (they need to be green and fresh – in the spring, no good later in the year; take rubber gloves, scissors).

Lentil and bacon soup

A delicious and very nutritious start to a meal, sometimes with a topping of grated *cheese* or other topping. Nice without the bacon too.

Bean soups

There are a myriad ways of producing these, just be sure to use *cooked* beans (easy from tins), not raw where you'd find yourself having to soak and boil them for hours.

A nice idea for an unusual and superlatively healthy pulse soup is to bring a tin of beans (e g kidney or haricot or mixed) to the boil in water, milk or stock, then liquidise *half* (not all) while still hot, and return it to the pan; you end up with an interesting, easy and unusual thick soup.

French onion soup

This takes patience but is basically very easy. Slice the onions (fresh or frozen) into rings and cook in *butter* very very very slowly (that's the patience bit – you can do something else while you're waiting) for 40 minutes to an hour till they turn a lovely dark brown (not burnt) colour and caramelised.

(Sssh – if you don't have the time or the patience to wait, just cook them over a higher heat, even let them burn a little, then add marmite – not quite so perfect but pretty good all the same).

Add *stock* or (best) *wine*, additional *seasoning* and flavouring if wished, and bring slowly to the boil. Serve with *grated cheese* and a piece of toasted *French bread* on top. Almost a meal in itself.

SOME SUMMER SOUPS

Lettuce summer soup

Cook and liquidise the lettuce in *chicken stock*. As it cools down beat an egg (unseparated, then carefully pour it into the lettuce mix.

Gazpacho

This is the best known summer soup, with lots of different recipes. You can use just about any leftover *salad*, but my favourite is sliced *red onion, cucumber, sweet peppers, tomatoes* (lots), *good quality olive oil* (this is important), a little *red wine*, some torn up pieces of stale *bread,* ground *cumin,* generous *sea salt* and ground *black pepper*, liquidise (or sieve) till very smooth, chill in fridge for several hours and serve cold. Everyone's turns out different, but always special.

Vichyssoise

This is the most famous cold soup of all, and rightly so. To the normal base add chopped *leek* and *lemon juice,* liquidise till very very smooth. Serve cold. A great start to a formal dinner party.

Banana and rum soup

Use ripe or over-ripe, bananas, mix with a bit of rum and a lot of *cream*. Liquidise till smooth but still thick.

THIN SOUPS

I do sometimes cook thin soups. The best and properest way is of course to make your own stock, typically from meat and/or bones bought specially for this purpose, perhaps plus some vegetables and seasoning to taste: nothing really beats that. But I've also found that, contrary to what I had initially assumed, using a packet soup as the basis for starting things off can work pretty well (as a busy working mother, I'd leave it to soak in cold water during the day while I was at work). So does a good quality stock *cube. You can* finish it off with some marmite or oxo to give the personal touch, plus some fairly finely chopped *vegetables* – frozen peas are the easiest but really any – and/or some pasta like macaroni pieces, and maybe a splash of wine, any kind, then bring the lot to a simmer.

As a good-bad cook you'll have no problem building on these examples. There are infinite variations on these basics.

SOUP TOPPINGS

These make a real difference to a dish's reception (and we good-bad cooks know well that *looks* as well as tastes matter).

Swirls of cream or yoghurt look good, or dollops of thicker cream, also herbs, either whole or chopped (I specially like mint, parsley or chives), seeds, nuts (walnuts look very good on top), or cheese (specially on French onion or lentil soups). And here's a nice idea to top parsnip or, indeed, any cream soup. Peel small strips of *parsnip* (potato peeler), fry quickly till brown and crispy: they curl into fantastic shapes and if put on a bit of kitchen paper for an hour or so will stay crisp, and look spectacular on top of the soup.

On the side

This helps the soup too:

- Your own soda bread (nice to cut it at table), oatcakes or toasted potato bread..
- French long loaf, cut diagonally two thirds of the way through into thick, semi-slices and buttered (with garlic if wished), then heated quickly in a hot oven.
- Butter in a lordly dish with a fancy butter knife for people to help themselves.

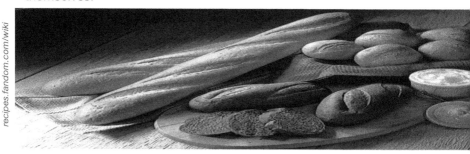

recipes.fandom.com/wiki

Chapter 6:
BEANS, FISH, MEAT, AND TWO–LEGS

In some parts of the world (but not all) meat has been regarded as an important, even essential, part of the expected diet. Most cookery books devote a large proportion of their entries to meat. Recently, it seems to have become less central even for non-vegetarians. However it is still important in many cuisines so needs some attention here.

Meat for Humans

It is often assumed that meat, hunted down then eaten raw, was *the* central food of early humans – " red in tooth and claw". But in fact (this was a surprise to me too) the diet of the earliest humans was probably similar to that of other great apes and of modern chimpanzees: omnivorous, including large quantities of forest fruit, leaves, flowers, bark, seeds, nuts, roots, insects (the evidence for this comes from the archaeological study of teeth). They ate little or no meat and, not yet with tools, i.e. with weapons to enable them to hunt, what meat they did consume came from what they could scavenge from animals killed by other predators.

Then came climate change. The forests shrank and way to grasslands and more herbivores, so there was a turn to hunting rather than relying solely on gathering and scavenging in the forests. Humans, it seems, adopted meat as a dietary staple much earlier than once thought.

This was a historic step. It not only went along with the development of hand-cut weapons such as hafted stone points but, equally important, for the hunting of large animals such as bison or deer bands of *several* people working together were needed: *cooperation* developed as a key, and necessary, human quality.

So around two and a half million years ago there was a dramatic expansion in humans' food as some began incorporating meat and marrow into their diet (we know because of the butchery marks in fossil bones). This marked a sharp divergence between humans and other primates (and animals generally) in the human use of flaked stone tools to access the animal meat and – remarkable when you think about it – in the ability to obtain food from animals much larger than themselves.

In time the establishment of settlements during the Neolithic Revolution allowed the domestication of animals such as chickens, sheep, rabbits, pigs, and cattle, dating back to the end of the last glacial period (c. 10,000 BC). This allowed the systematic production of meat and the selective breeding of animals for this purpose, going along with a liking for to *cooked* food.

Poultry

Roast chicken

Any kind of poultry ("two legs") is good roasted: chicken, duck, turkey – all very popular – or, not so easy to find nowadays, goose (something I specially love: when I was a child roast goose was always cooked for my birthday on New Year's Eve).

Rub some *olive oil, salt* and *pepper* into the skin and, to save time later, add some thickening like oats or small bits of potato in the roasting tin (then you'll have near-ready gravy when it's done); roast in a moderately hot oven, roughly following any timing from your butcher or the packaging, and in any case till the skin is brown and crisp and no blood appears when you pierce a thigh with a skewer. I don't bother with basting – it's not needed if you've oiled the skin well and just results in opening the oven and letting the heat out – but it's worth checking about two-thirds of the way through to make sure the breast isn't getting too brown; if so cover lightly with a piece of foil.

Potatoes and/or other root *vegetables* are good roasted alongside the fowl. A cut *apple* or *orange* adds a nice contrasting flavour either beside the bird, or put inside to keep the roast moist, and *herbs* like rosemary or thyme sprinkled on the breast or tucked behind the joints add to the looks and flavour. It is lovely served with *redcurrant jelly, bread sauce* or (my favourite with just about anything) *puréed apple/apple sauce.*

CHICKEN HISTORY

Chicken is the most common type of poultry in the world, partly owing to the relative ease and low cost of raising chickens compared to mammals such as cattle or pigs.

The chickens of today are descended from wild junglefowl hybrids first domesticated thousands of years ago in south-east Asia. This seems to have happened in the early second millennium BC, going along with the cultivation of rice and millet which attracted the wild fowl to human settlements.

This eventuated in their dispersal across the globe. In the second millennium, domesticated chickens spread to Central Chins, South Asia, and Mesopotamia, then to Ethiopia and Mediterranean Europe. In ancient Egypt by the mid-15th century BC, they were dubbed "the bird that gives birth every day". Chicken then came to be one of the most common meats available in the Middle Ages, spread to the Americas, and is with us, worldwide, as a regular and highly acceptable part of our cooked diet today.

Curry hurry

Gently fry some sliced *onion* with a good *mix of curry spices* to taste (alternatively with ready prepared curry paste or curry powder), add chopped *chicken* pieces and a *tin of cream soup* (eg chicken, celery, or mushroom soup, undiluted if condensed), and simmer for ten minutes. Serve with *rice, mango chutney,* and/or *Greek yoghurt*, plus if wished (bought) *papadums*.

Curry hurry best

Make the above into a feast by adding a proliferation of side dishes in separate bowls for people to help themselves, such as sliced bananas, oranges or other fruit; nuts; seeds; dried coconut; sliced tomatoes, radishes, peppers, cucumber; in fact *anything and everything* you have in. It will look impressive – clearly you have made a real effort!!

This was the common Sunday lunch in Indian colonial days, accompanied (but you don't need to do this) by bottles of hard liquor on the side. It still makes for a lovely buffet occasion, a real show.

Chicken pilau

For once it's important to get the proportions right: one measure of *rice* (preferably long grained) to two of *stock* so that there is the right amount of liquid for the rice to absorb.

Gently fry together, stirring, *rice, chopped onion, garlic* if wished, *spices* to taste (such as cloves, cinnamon, cumin, cardamom, and turmeric) and chopped *cooked chicken* until well mixed and fragrant (about 5 minutes). Add stock and simmer for about 5 minutes.

FIRST ROAST MEAT

Transfer to a covered oven dish and cook in a moderate low oven till the rice has absorbed the liquid (about 30 minutes). Fluff up the rice with a fork, stir in some raisins, and top with flaked almonds.

This is also good if instead of chicken you use bacon, salmon, leeks or – well (it's after all an adaptable peasant dish) anything you have lying around. Any left overs heat up well too.

OTHER MEAT

I mostly go for poultry. "Two legs good, four legs bad" was what I was once told by a Ghanaian foot expert on a cruise, and I suppose that's nutritionally true. But for a special occasion once in a while I rather like four legs like lamb, beef or pork. Good quality cuts can be roasted in the same way as poultry, while stewing and casseroling (below) are good ways to cook red meat, including the cheap tougher cuts.

Top fry

Fry chopped ham, bacon or other meat with chopped vegetables (like onions, peas and/or sweet peppers) fresh herbs and if you wish a sprinkle of oats and/or cheese. You can't get much simpler than this and it tastes great.

Rack of lamb

Rub freshly ground sea *salt, pepper, rosemary* and/or other *herbs* into lamb ribs, drizzle with *olive oil* and leave for a little to absorb the flavours. Roast uncovered in a very hot oven (about 15 minutes for pink meat (my preference), longer if you like your meat well done). Good served with mint or redcurrant sauce.

A great dinner party dish that's easy and always special.

Skewer delight

Soak 2-inch (or so) cubes of *beef* in a marinade of *red wine, olive oil, garlic and herbs* for 3-4 hours or overnight, string on skewers interspersed with *mushrooms, small onions* and pieces of *sweet pepper,* brush with the marinade and cook in very high oven (tray under to catch drips), grill, or barbecue till well browned. One skewer per person.

Ham superlative

Cook a handful of noodles or other *pasta* till tender. Mix these with chopped leftover ham or other cooked *meat, sweet pepper, and a tin of thick cream soup,* top with *breadcrumbs* dotted with *butter* and/or *grated cheese* and bake uncovered in a moderate oven till topping is crisp (about 30-40 minutes).

Beef stroganoff

Gently fry a chopped *onion* till soft but not brown, ideally in *butter*, together with sliced *button mushrooms*, then add a good quantity of rump or fillet *beef* cut (against the grain) into thin strips, flattened and seasoned with *black pepper, nutmeg* and *mace,* fry for 5 minutes turning so the strips are all browned, add ½ pt *soured cream* and heat through. Serve immediately.

CASSEROLES

Casseroles are great family staples: warming, easy, economical and people-friendly. They're great for preparing the day before, also good for reheating any leftovers and still looking good. They can be done in the oven or slow cooker or simmered slowly in a heavy saucepan on top of the cooker (then generally referred to as stews); I personally think that method needs more attention and that the flavours do not blend so well but some people prefer it.

Slow cooker casserole

Slow cookers are extremely convenient: you just sling everything in to-gether – chunks of meat, root vegetables, onions, seasoning, other flavouring (herbs, spices, marmite, soy sauce or whatever), maybe a little dried fruit or dark sugar, thickening (red lentils are good – very healthy and effective), and stock or wine to just cover, switch on, then leave the cooker to get on with it, no further attention needed. Cook for several hours, all day or (set at low) overnight. Even cheap potentially tough meat becomes tender and delicious and the mix ends up with a wonderfully mature, blended, taste.

Venison and bacon casserole

Fry chunks of venison, bacon, chopped *onion*, and *root vegetables* such as turnip/swede, carrots and/or parsnips, till brown, then transfer to oven dish. Add *seasoning*, *herbs* such as thyme, parsley, bay leaf, a couple of tablespoons of *redcurrant or rowan jelly*, *oats* or *mashed potato* to thicken, then cover with *stock or wine* and cook, covered, in a moderate oven till tender (about an hour and a half). Serve with potatoes. This basic casserole treatment can be varied almost infinitely, using whatever meat, vegetables, flavouring and liquid you prefer. Very nutritious and generally a great favourite with families.

Ground nut stew

Cook as above adding pieces of chicken or other meat but for flavouring and thickening add half or a whole jar of good quality peanut butter. The nutty sauce makes an unusually delicious, tasty, and highly nutritious meal. Alternatively throw everything into a slow cooker and leave to cook on medium for several hours. Without the meat this also makes a good vegetarian option, with, if you wish, the addition of hard boiled eggs, one or two per person, stirred into the mix before serving.

(I use bought peanut butter, but of course if you want the authentic way, go to Africa, dig up the peanuts (they grow underground and are actually legumes rather than nuts proper), shell then roast them, pound them to a paste, and use the result for the stew. Like me you may prefer the buy-a-jar method).

Coq au vin

This is actually just a version of chicken casserole – but it somehow sounds better with a French name (blame the Normans and their upper-class "cuisine"). Originally it used an old tough rooster (the "coq") so don't bother searching out the most expensive chicken in the shop when going for this recipe, just cook it long and slow.

It is delicious and for a famous classic dish not as difficult to prepare as you might think, so though takes a bit longer and more care than some dishes it's worth it.

So here goes.

Reduce a bottle of *red wine* (ideally pinot noir, burgundy, or the like) to half by boiling it down, meanwhile fry lightly till brown roughly chopped *bacon* (ideally Italian pancetta or smoked back), *pearl onions* if you can get them (otherwise thickly sliced regular onions), *garlic*, and *button mushrooms*. Add the reduced wine and enough good-quality *stock* (chicken or, surprisingly effective , *beef stock*) to cover, a little *tomato purée* (for the colour), *lentils* (for thickening, ideally to a medium thin gravy), mixed *herbs* and *seasoning*. Bake in a covered pot in a moderate oven for about 45 minutes or until chicken is tender (alternatively several hours in a slow cooker). The flavours develop and deepen if left till the next day. Nice served with mashed potatoes.

History of alcohol in cooking

Ethanol, the alcohol found in beverages, made its way into our kitchens as early as 4000 BC when humans first discovered the process of fermentation. Fermented foods, like bread and cheese, were the first examples of ethanol's culinary usage. As civilisation evolved, so did the mastery of fermentation, leading to the production of alcoholic beverages like wine, beer, and mead.

Ethanol, the alcohol found in beverages, made its way into our kitchens as early as the Neolithic period (around 4000 BC), when humans first discovered the process of fermentation. Fermented foods, like bread and cheese, were the first examples of ethanol's culinary usage. As time went on people became increasingly expert in the processes of fermentation, leading to the production of alcoholic beverages like wine, beer, and mead. The earliest definitely known alcoholic beverage in the world, in about 7000 BC, was a fermented drink of rice, honey, hawthorn fruit and grape, but alcohol may well have been known before that.

The Renaissance was a pivotal era for alcohol in cooking. The distillation process was refined, leading to the production of spirits – high-proof alcohols like brandy, whiskey, and rum. These potent beverages began to find their way into the culinary world. Cooks realised that, in addition to their intoxicating effects, these spirits could also enhance the flavour of dishes.

Alcohol has many culinary uses in bringing out the full taste of flavours, preserving food, and even putting on a show with techniques like flambé. So, the next time you use alcohol in your cooking, you'll appreciate not just its utility but also its spirited history.

Fish and seafood

Fish have even fewer legs, none in fact, so no doubt extra good for you. Certainly they are the basis for many fine fishy meals.

Fishy facts

Few places are totally without access to some kind of water – rivers, lakes, sea and so fish was probably an earlier regular food than meat, being easier and considerably less dangerous to catch (no huge beasts bigger than yourself to overcome). Presumably first consumed raw, it doubtless was found to be even more pleasant baked in the embers of a fire or hung over a dying fire in times of relative plenty to be smoked or dried, so as to be preserved against later scarcity.

Haddock kedgeree

A classic comfort dish of haddock, egg and rice, ready in 40 minutes. Fry gently in butter a finely chopped *onion, a little curry powder* or *spices* (cardamon, cinnamon, bay leaves and turmeric are good), then add *peas* and a good handful of *rice* (ideally basmati), stir till it's all well mixed, then cover with chicken *stock* and/or *white wine*, simmer over low heat till the rice is tender, add flaked *haddock*, roughly chopped hard-boiled *eggs, chopped parsley* and *seasoning,* bring up to heat again and serve hot with *lemon* wedges.

Kedgeree history

Kedgeree started off as a breakfast dish, but nowadays is mostly eaten as a main meal. In India in colonial times it was served to the British for breakfast and the recipe then brought back from India by returning soldiers, missionaries and colonial officials who introduced it to Victorian Britain.

Simple salmon

The "king of fishes" can be cooked in a myriad ways – fried, baked (not too long), lightly roasted, in pies, simmered, or, for a celebration, whole. Here is the simplest:

Flake a tin or tins of salmon, mix with *peas,* chopped *tomato* and *mayonnaise. Serve* with boiled new *potatoes* and *butter* or with *parsley* sauce.

Salmon pie

Put roughly cubed salmon fillets, chopped *celery, parsley, peas* and if wished *prawns* into an oven dish, cover with mashed *potato.* Bake uncovered in a moderately hot oven until the top is crispy and golden (about 30 minutes).

Bacon scallops

I don't go hugely for shellfish – fiddly to prepare, and, to me, the taste isn't worth the effort. However *scallops* can be lovely.

Fry strips of *bacon* till crisp, and in another pan fry *scallops* quickly on each side. Top the cooked scallops with the bacon in a serving dish scattered with toasted or fried *breadcrumbs* and chopped *parsley*, with *lemon* wedges on the side.

BEANS

There are a huge number of beans (pulses) to choose from and they are great for the good-bad cook - well, for any cook, even the good-good ones provided you use the precooked variety (conveniently in tins). They're also perfect for non-meat-eating vegetarians, even, mostly, for vegans.

Casseroles, including those above, are also delicious if beans are substituted for meat, it is only the *names* that are changed. A couple of rather special ones are:

Italian bean casserole

Tip into a heavy saucepan, casserole, oven dish, or slow cooker chopped *celery, carrots, leeks, garlic, lemon zest, thyme, tomatoes* (fresh, chopped, or tinned), *red lentils, tinned ready-prepared beans* of any kind (the main ingredient) and *wine* or *stock*. Simmer, covered, for about an hour.

Chilli con carne

Fry chopped *onions, tomatoes (sun dried* is nicest but any will do), *oregano, garlic, spices, chilli pepper* and *minced beef* till the meat is brown. Transfer into an oven dish, add *tinned kidney beans*, cover with *stock* and cook, covered, in moderate oven for 30-40 minutes. Alternatively cook for several hours in a slow cooker. Good served with avocado, and rice or pasta, with Greek yoghurt on the table for anyone who might find it a bit too spicy.

There are now excellent chilli con carne packet mixes for the flavouring which, added to your basic mix (but without the chilli pepper), can make just as nice, or nicer, a result, so why not (that's what it is to be a good bad cook, and anyway the children always loved it). Just follow the directions on the packet.

Baked beans

Though these are jokingly looked down on, haricot beans in tomato sauce, which is what they are, are an excellent and delicious food and very good for you, so take them seriously. They don't need further cooking, just heating up. They can be served on toast, as part of a mixed grill, or as an accompaniment to any kind of meat. Specially nice with bacon and – they're haricot beans after all – good for you too.

By now you may not be looking for easy dishes, but don't ignore baked beans on that account.

BAKED BEANS FROM THE PAST

Baked beans probably originated not in France, as some historians believe, but among Native American peoples in northeast America. The Iroquois and others mixed beans, maple sugar, and bear fat in earthenware pots and left this in underground pits called "bean holes" lined with hot rocks to cook slowly over a long time.

British colonists in New England learned about the dish from native peoples – maybe it reminded them of the pease porridge from home – and adapted it to their own culture. They used sugar instead of maple syrup and bacon or ham instead of bear fat, and simmered the beans for hours in pots over a fire instead of underground. They used different beans according to what was available locally.

In time the process became industrialised and largely standardised to be the now familiar Heinz tins of haricot beans cooked in a rich tomato sauce. By the early twentieth century tins of baked beans were trusted enough as a superlatively nutritious and convenient food to have been taken on Scott's Antarctic expedition, and they were and are consumed in huge numbers, especially in Britain and India.

Broad beans in parsley sauce

Simmer broad beans till tender (time will vary according to their size and maturity), serve with plentiful parsley sauce – amazingly filling and nourishing, and one of my toppest, simplest, favourites.

Lentil moussaka

Moussaka, originally a Greek dish, is traditionally made with minced lamb, but I think this vegetarian alternative is even nicer, as well as healthier.

Roast slices of *aubergine* in a moderate oven till soft and brown (about 20 minutes), meanwhile fry chopped *onions, tomatoes, courgettes,* and *spices* of choice (nutmeg specially nice) plus if wished other vegetables and *spices* of choice, when nearly soft add the aubergine and *red lentils.* Swirl around then transfer to an uncovered oven dish. Cover with *stock* or, as I prefer, *red wine,* plus some *tomato sauce.*

Before putting in the oven top with the traditional moussaka finish – a thick sauce, made by heating several tablespoons of *yoghurt, grated cheese,* and *nutmeg*; when hot, quickly stir in two gently beaten *eggs* – this helps the sauce to stay on top – take off the heat at once and pile on top of the mix. Cook uncovered in a moderate oven till the top is golden and puffy (about 30 minutes). If you like extra crunch, top further with *bread crumbs* and dabs of *butter* before baking.

BEAN FACTS

Beans are among the earliest cultivated plants in history, first, it seems, gathered in Afghanistan and the Himalayan foothills. Broad beans, also called fava beans, are in their wild state only the size of a small fingernail, An early cultivated form were grown in Thailand from the early seventh millennium BC and in ancient Egypt beans were deposited among other goods with the dead. Cultivated large-seeded beans began to be grown in the second millennium BC in the Aegean, Iberia, and transalpine Europe. In the Americas it originated in Mesoamerica, and subsequently spread southward, along with maize and squash, traditional companion crops.

CHAPTER 7:

AFTERS, THE UNNECESSARY, PERFECT, FINISH

Why not! And lots can be made beforehand or quickly and easily at the last minute. They fill up any cracks and make a pleasing, ritual-like, ending.

Soufflé omelette

Anything called soufflé sounds grand and difficult but this method is actually stupendously quick and easy.

Separate two *eggs* and mix the yolks lightly. Beat the whites till fluffy, then fold gently into the yolks. Fry quickly in *butter* in a hot pan until the bottom is just set (only a couple of minutes). Lift out carefully onto a plate (hopefully in one piece, but never mind if it breaks it will taste just the same). If it's for several people (with more eggs) divide it into wedges in the pan. Serve topped with dabs of *raspberry jam, honey, crunchy sugar* or other flavouring (even, to turn it into a savoury lunch dish, finely grated *cheese*).

The recipe books say you should go on to seal the top before serving by it putting under a grill or in a hot oven but personally I think it looks, feels and tastes nicer and more delicate left fluffy and soft on top.

Rum bananas

Very quick and easy. Gently fry quartered *bananas, rum* and *sugar* in *butter*, plus if wished a little *lemon juice.* Serve with *cream* and more sprinkled sugar (ideally brown, crunchy).

Fruit and cream delight

Slice *fresh fruit* such as peach, banana or mango and sprinkle liberally with *crunchy brown sugar,* then serve in separate bowls with *cream, Greek yoghurt,* or *ice cream.*

Carageen jelly

An interesting and unusual dessert.

Rinse a handful of *dried carageen seaweed* in a sieve under a cold tap. In a saucepan cover it with ample cold water, simmer till it begins to thicken, take off the heat, strain through a fine sieve pushing the jelly well through. Add melted *chocolate* or *cocoa powder* blended with water and *brown sugar*, then *milk* to get the desired consistency and taste (amounts are trial and error as they depend on how gelatinous the carageen is; keep the seaweed handy in case you need to thicken it a bit more). Eventually give it a good whisk to aerate and lighten it and chill in the fridge. Serve with *brown sugar* and *cream*.

You can vary it by omitting the chocolate and if you wish adding a drop of colouring (pink looks nice), thus retaining carageen's distinctive, mild, flavour.

It can also be varied by adding some runny honey to the mix, a whipped cream topping, a variety of sauces, or the addition of an egg yolk beaten into the jelly before it sets with the egg white either folded into the jelly or whisked into a soft meringue topping.

SEAWEED FOR HUMANS?

Plants are found in every sea and ocean. From the equator to the poles, vast beds of seaweeds grow from just above the beach line to the furthest depths that light reaches, a vast and diverse group of ancient aquatic plants. It is no wonder that the impact of seaweeds is ancient and substantial, going back at least 20,000 years. No fewer than nine species of seaweed and marine algae have been found by archaeologists in the hearths of the most ancient human settlements known in the Americas and in Europe. Seaweed has in fact been part

of the human diet for millennia, from as early as the Mesolithic, through the Neolithic transition, and into recent years. There is good reason for this for – perhaps surprisingly – seaweed is higher in vitamins and minerals than any other type of food. It is strong in minerals and protein and a good source of digestible fibre.

There are scores of varieties of edible seaweeds. One example is dulse, a dried seaweed popular in Ireland and among Irish immigrants in America (commonly served as a nibble in pubs). Another is agar, widely used as a gelling agent in yoghurt and jam, plus several others popular in Japanese cooking.

The carrageen (literally "little rock") seaweed that you've read about here is currently the best known in Europe and America. Since it comes from western Ireland it is very much part of my own upbringing. It is a brownish-black or dark green seaweed from 3-6 inches long that grows abundantly on rocks along the low tide line off the south and west coasts of Ireland. It is rich in iodine and trace elements and full of natural gelatine.

Since it grows very close to the sea level it can only be reached at the lowest spring tides and collecting even a few sprigs of it is a significantly dangerous process. Well do I remember my mother, afraid of nothing, going off to gather it; not until I was grown up did I realise how perilous those slippery rocks and clutching waves really were – but, being her, she always came back smiling with a load of the seaweed she was after.

Once gathered the carageen is left out to bleach in the sun till white and dry, then, traditionally, stored for up to two years in a jute bag. Now it can be bought in health food shops and some supermarkets.

TRADITIONAL HOT FAMILY PUDDINGS

Queen of puddings (well named)

Mix a good handful of *bread crumbs, egg yolks,* **and** *sugar* in an oven dish, pour over hot *milk* to cover and leave till the crumbs have been absorbed (about 20 minutes). Spread with softened (warm) *jam*, then top with meringue from the *egg whites and* cook in a medium low oven till lightly browned (about 30 minutes). For a softer meringue topping add it just for the last 10 minutes.

Bread pudding

Bread? That sounds heavy, but it is actually surprisingly light and delicate. Lay layers of buttered *slightly old bread* (you can also use tea loaf or cake) with *raisins* or other *dried fruit,* and *cinnamon, ginger* or other *spice* in an oven dish, pour over beaten–together eggs and milk, leave for a while to soak, then cook uncovered in a moderate oven till firm and golden (about an hour).

Burnt orange

Sprinkle thin rounds or half rounds of *orange* (skin on) with *brandy* or *other spirit and/*or a *spice* such as ginger or cinnamon; if time allows leave to soak, then sprinkle with *brown sugar*, heat under a hot grill or in oven till burnt round the edges. Serve either hot or left to cool and harden, with *cream*.

Enchanted grapefruit

A variation of the above: sprinkle *red or pink grapefruit* halves with *sugar* and, if you wish, a dash of *brandy* or *rum*, grill until brown and caramelised, eat hot. This also makes a great and very quick starter.
Fruit brûlée

Slice some *fruit* (fresh, frozen, or from a drained tin) such as peaches, apricots, raspberries, blackberries, cover with a thick layer of *Greek yoghurt* or *whipped cream,* then smother with a further layer of *brown sugar.* Heat under a hot grill till the sugar melts and caramelises. Leave to cool and harden before eating.

Lemon surprise

Separate yolks and whites of 2 *eggs*. Cream together 2oz butter and 4oz *sugar*, add zest and juice of two *lemons*, beat in egg yolks, then 2oz *oats* and 5 fl oz *milk*. Whisk the egg whites in a separate bowl till stiff, then fold lightly into the lemon batter. Pour into an uncovered oven dish and cook in a moderate oven until golden brown (40-45 minutes). It ends up with a fluffy sponge above and – the surprise – the tangy lemon sauce below.

Lemon meringue pie, the all–time favourite

Separate two *eggs*. Whisk together 2 oz *sugar*, 2 oz softened *butter*, 3 tablespoonfuls *cornflour*, 2 *lemons* (whole) liquidised, plus a little water (not too much – the amount depends on the size and liquidity of the lemons) so as to make a creamy mix. Whisk in the beaten egg yolks and pour the mixture into a *pastry case* (bought or from home-made pastry or biscuit crust). Beat the egg whites till foamy, add 4oz *caster sugar* and beat till it has stiff peaks. Spread this (not too smoothly) over the lemon mixture, making sure it reaches the sides of the pastry case, and cook in a moderate oven till top is light brown and the meringue topping crisp on top (about 20 minutes). Serve cold, with *cream*.

Baked custard

Beat together 3 eggs, a tablespoon sugar, and 8fl oz hot milk till smooth. Cook uncovered, topped if wished with a sprinkle of nutmeg, in microwave for 10-12 minutes, (stirring once half way through) or moderate oven (30 minutes), till loosely set. This method is simpler and more reliable than the traditional all-stirring desperately-avoiding-a-curdle saucepan version.

Rice pudding

The simplest hot dessert of all (though to be honest not *everyone* likes it – I cook it all the same!). Put a handful of *rice* (best is pudding rice but any will do) in an uncovered oven dish, cover with *milk* (two cupfuls to one cupful of rice) plus, if you have it, some *cream*, cook in a moderate oven for about an hour and a half or until it has a light brown skin on top. You can just forget about it till you're ready to eat, no need to stir or keep checking. Nice on its own but before putting it in the oven you can add flavourings such as *nutmeg* (grated on top) or other *spice*, or (to me best) *raisins*. It looks and tastes extra good served with a spoonful of *jam* on top.

Apple pie

Put sliced peeled apples plus *sugar* and *spices* (e g cinnamon) to taste in an uncovered oven dish, cover with your chosen topping and cook till the top is slightly brown, the apple tender. This also works well with other fruit such as plums, pears, apricots or (a regular favourite) blackberry and apple; also nice with well sweetened rhubarb.

TOPPINGS FOR FRUIT PIES – ADD BEFORE BAKING

- **Pastry** – buy frozen, then follow package instructions
- **Charlotte** – mix breadcrumbs (main ingredient) with sugar and a little butter, plus spices if wished
- **Crumble** – rub together approximately equal amounts of oats, butter and sugar until it feels like coarse breadcrumbs
- **Cake mixture** – beat together handful of oats, handful of sugar and two eggs plus spices to taste (cinnamon and/or ginger are good
- **Meringue** – egg white(s) beaten with sugar till stiff enough to stand up in soft peaks.
- **Corn flakes** (an immense variety to choose from – don't overcook, they're not so nice burnt).

PUDDINGS IN HISTORY

Unlike other foods described here, puddings as such are relatively recent and are not found in all regional cuisines.

The first "puddings" made by ancient cooks were similar to sausages: our word in fact comes from the Middle English "poding" which meant a "meat filled" animal stomach. In Homer's Odyssey we hear of a blood pudding roasted in a pig's stomach, and mediaeval puddings were mostly meat–based. In 17th century England puddings were either savoury (meat–based) or sweet (flour, nuts and sugar), boiled in special pudding bags. The "pease porridge" of the old nursery rhyme was probably a simple boiled pudding of pease meal (meal made from yellow field peas). By the later 18th century traditional English puddings no longer included meat while 19th century puddings were still boiled but ended more like rich fruit cake, still traditionally served around Christmas as plum pudding.

A contrasting tradition was custard in its various forms. Ancient Roman cooks like Alpicius (said to have invented egg custard) knew about the binding properties of eggs and created many egg-based dishes such as savoury custards, custard tarts and omelettes; these could be either savoury (made with cheese, meat, pepper) or sweet (with honey, nuts, cinnamon).

Our present–day sweet custard dates from the Middle Ages when custard was eaten on its own or as a filling for pies and tarts. It was a dish very popular at the time: the word "custard" comes from a reference to the pastry "crust" of the tart.

Irish coffee

This is just hot strong coffee with a good dash of *whiskey* or other *spirit* or *liqueur* (brandy for "French coffee", rum for "Jamaican" …) served very hot topped with whipped *cream* or with pouring cream (pour over the back of a teaspoon to keep it on the surface). There are speciality glasses to show it off but any heat resistant mug will do fine. This is a great choice to end a meal, either after everything else or in place of the afters course. It has several advantages:

* It can easily be varied – and without fuss – to suit people who want caffeinated or decaffeinated, alcoholic or not.
* It's fine on its own but can be dressed up to look extra–luxurious with macaroons, biscuits or chocolates on the side.
* Despite the coffee, it seems to make people sleepy so they don't linger too long, and
* There's almost no washing up afterwards.

Turkish coffee – very special

Measure two tablespoonfuls per person of strong, high quality, very finely *ground coffee* (if possible the Mehmet Efendi blend) into a *cezve*, a Turkish copper coffee pot (if not available use a heavy saucepan) plus – but only if wanted – *sugar*. Add one and a half cupfuls of water per each person's cup, stir once, and heat slowly without further stirring. Do not let it boil. It will start to foam up, when the foam reaches right up (2-3 minutes), take off the heat and pour carefully into each cup making sure all the foam is transferred as this is an essential part of the drink. The experience of drinking Turkish coffee demands that it should be made a beautiful occasion, both the pouring out ceremoniously from the *cezve* and the placing of a glass of cold water each (the coffee is very strong) plus an attractive side dish of *Turkish delight* and/or honeyed *baklava*. It is drunk very hot.

The small straight-sided cups commonly used are part of the occasion, as is the foam. Another tradition is to follow up the drink with fortune telling based on the foam left at the bottom of the cups (let's hope the foam foresees a bright future for this book and, more important, for its readers!)

Coffee in history

Coffee drinking began in the Ottoman Empire in the early 15th century in the form of "Turkish coffee" as found in Yemen in the Arabian peninsula, probably one of the oldest forms of coffee brewing in the world. In one story of its origin the Yemen Ottoman governor was so impressed by the products of the local coffee brewers in the ports he visited that he persuaded the Sultan to give it his seal of approval and it spread around the whole empire. Or perhaps it was that in the late fifteenth century Syrian traders arrived in Istanbul, and opened coffee shops around the city modelled on Yemeni coffee houses. The Ottoman Sultan visited, loved the drink – and the rest is history!

Whatever the actual origin – and it is hard to imagine its wide spread without some endorsement from the Sultan – it caught on, its importance and speciality preparation rated so high that a woman's marital prospects are said to have turned on her coffee-making skills.

The subsequent spread of the coffee plant throughout the world was, as with many other food stuffs, helped on by the age of exploration, especially by the Dutch who brought it to their trading partners in India and Asia. The French were particularly influential in introducing the plant to the Americas but other colonial powers also played a part. The earliest cultivating of coffee in the New World was probably the result of Gabriel de Clieu bringing coffee seedlings to Martinique in 1720. This enabled its spread to other Caribbean islands and to Mexico.

By 1852 Brazil had become the world's largest producer of coffee – we've all heard of "all the coffee in Brazil" – though several other major producers have also developed, notably in Colombia, the Ivory Coast, Ethiopia, and Vietnam.

By now modern production techniques have made coffee a worldwide household item used not only as a drink but as a popular flavouring in cooking.

AFTERTHOUGHTS

Fresh fruit

A bit of a cheat in *this* book as it doesn't involve cooking or other kitchen preparation, but both pleasant and easy.

Apples are always great favourites. Good dessert apples are lovely eaten just as they are, but there is also a large range of *exotic fruits* to choose from such as figs, guavas (one of my favourites), grapes and persimmons.

Apple history

Apples are almost certainly our oldest eaten fruit as approximately 750,000 years ago early Stone Age food gatherers in central Asia discovered sour crab apples growing wild in the forest. By about 8,000 years ago, Neolithic farmers in Asia were apparently *cultivating* these wild apples. We know a bit more about what happened later. In 1300 BC Egyptians were planting orchards along the Nile Delta, while in 800 BC ancient Greeks were – impressively – already using grafting techniques.

When the Romans conquered England in the first century BC they planted orchards where apples have flourished ever since in a multiplicity of ever widening varieties, both humanly contrived and self generating.

They were brought to Mexico and South America by Spaniards in the 1500s. By the 1600s apples had made their way to North America too. Crab apples preceded European colonists to America, but as the fruit was not very edible, seeds and cuttings were brought out from England and in time every farm in the Americas, as in Europe. was growing apples.

They have stayed favourites all through recorded history, not just for their widespread symbolic associations but for their continuing vibrant uses for both cooking and eating raw.

How unfair that Eve is *blamed* – just look what she got for us!

Oxford high table dessert

In beautiful serving platters, plus individual plates on the side for people to help themselves, lay out a selection of luxury quality *dried fruit* (e g dates, prunes, figs, either as they are or, specially wonderful, caramelised from having been heated coated with *butter* and *sugar or honey*), *nuts in their shells* (remember nutcrackers), and *fine wine* or *liqueur* (port is the traditional favourite) and/or or some *exotic fruit drink*.

Ice cream

There is such a wide range of delicious varieties on sale that it's nowadays rather over-the-top to try making your (no harm if you want to of course). You can customise by mixing in a new flavouring (stem ginger or marmalade for example) or topping with your own sauce – see, you *are* a cook, one of the sensible good-bad getting-away-with-it brigade.

Cheese and biscuits

This is another satisfying and ritual-like end to a meal, all the better if the biscuits are your own home-made *oatcake*.

CHEESE IN HISTORY

Cheese was probably discovered by accident from the practice of storing milk in containers made from the stomachs of animals.

There is evidence of cheese-making over 5,000 years ago in the time of the First Dynasty of Egypt, depicted on Egyptian tomb murals. The art of cheesemaking is also referred to in ancient Greek mythology, and Roman soldiers were issued a daily cheese allowance, a tradition that continues in armies today.

In the Middle Ages the city of Damietta was famous for its soft, white cheese. Cheese was also imported, and the common hard yellow cheese, *rumi*, takes its name from the Arabic word for "Roman".

Chapter 8:
SAUCES, SPICES, SEASONINGS

Let me gather up a few bits and pieces which didn't quite fit earlier but a good-bad cook will want to know about.

SAUCES AND ACCOMPANIMENTS

Meat gravy

This is the traditional sauce made from the juices of a meat roast. But, if it's me, it so often burns, gets lumps, and is that most flustering of things – a last minute task when everyone is ready to sit down and you want to be cool and unhurried.

So what's really wrong with warming up a delicious gravy from a bought (high quality) packet, granules, or cube? Always have some handy.

First things (your smiling relaxed face) first: *that's* what family and friends want, not a flustered chef however brilliant!

Mayonnaise

Home made mayonnaise is pleasing and quite fun to make provided you have a bit of patience. All you have to do is very gradually (to avoid curdling) add a dripping teaspoon at a time from a half pint of slightly warm *oil* to two *egg yolks*, beating all the time; once it starts to thicken you can add the oil a bit more quickly, by the end pour it, still beating, in a thin steady stream till the mix is thick and yellow-y cream in colour, then gently stir in one or two teaspoons of *white wine vinegar* or *lemon juice*.

But again – now that you can buy first rate mayonnaise why bother! Just be sure to decant it into a beautiful-looking container. RESIST the common notion that the ability to make mayonnaise is the test of a proper, good, cook.

Hollandaise sauce

Melt 8oz *butter* until hot. In an electric blender/liquidiser beat three *egg yolks,* one teaspoon of *dijon mustard,* one tablespoon (about) of *lemon juice,* and a pinch of *cayenne pepper,* then, while blender is running, slowly stream in the hot butter and it's ready. Serve quickly while still hot.

Mint sauce

Chop mint leaves (either finely or coarsely, both are nice), release the flavour with a little *sugar* and a teaspoon or so of *boiling water,* then cover liberally with *white wine vinegar* or *lemon juice.* Traditionally served with lamb but why stick just to that?

Red magic

Mix *redcurrant sauce,* grated *orange peel,* and *chopped mint leaves.* That's it.

Orange sauce

Liquidise orange(s) (any kind but seville specially good for a bitter orange flavour) and combine with *stock* (from a chicken stock cube is fine), *sea salt* and *black pepper.* If too runny add a little *cornflour and warm. Pour over* some *port* or *red wine* to taste. Lovely complement to any meat, specially duck or pork.

Cumberland sauce

Gently warm *redcurrant jelly* (the main ingredient) and a bit of *port* till the jelly melts, take off heat and add thin strips of *orange* peel, juice of the orange, *ground ginger,* and a little *mustard powder.* Whisk together and serve cold. Nice with just about anything, specially cold turkey.

Anchovy butter

Liquidise or mash together *butter,* a drained *tin of anchovies, lemon juice,* and a (large or small to taste) pinch of cayenne pepper.

Herby butter

Mash butter (warm slightly if it's hard) with chopped *herbs* like chives, thyme (or, well, anything you like and happen to have), *lemon juice,* and salt and pepper. Infinitely variable.

Too often forgotten (because it's so easy?) this is lovely with just about anything (meat, pasta, pulse) and suggests the cook has really gone to trouble to make things appetising.

Lemon butter

Mix butter, lemon juice, and a little grated lemon peel.

Peanut sauce

Gently fry chopped *onion, ginger* and (if wished) *garlic,* then add *peanut butter* (main ingredient), *coconut cream* if available, *soy sauce, sugar, lemon juice,* and a touch of *chilli.* Simmer for a few minutes. Also nice as a dip.

Avocado sauce or dip

Mash together avocado flesh, lemon juice and sour cream or Greek yoghurt with generous seasoning.

MARINADES

Marinades – a juice in which you soak ingredients before cooking them – are an excellent way not only to bring out and deeply mingle the flavours you've chosen but also a way of making even the cheapest, roughest, toughest, meat tender and eatable. You can use any mix of oil and spices or herbs, but my favourite ones (always with a generous amount of seasoning) are:

* Wine or lemon juice, olive oil, garlic, herbs
* Soy sauce, olive oil, chopped onion, ginger
* Yoghurt (any kind), olive oil and spices. Specially good as a preparation for chicken tikka

Leave meat (chopped) to steep, covered, for at least an hour or, best, overnight in the fridge, then lift out the meat and cook in your normal way for the particular dish you're intending. A handy method is to soak in the marinade overnight in a switched-off slow cooker, then, still in the marinade, start it cooking the next morning.

SAUCES FOR DESSERTS

Pouring cream

Now that you can get long life cream that tastes as good as fresh you can always have some in the fridge. As a sauce it is every bit as delicious as any lengthily laboured over concoction, as well as having a multitude of uses.

Custard

This sometimes seems to be a bit of a test piece for a cook. You can use custard powder which is actually perfectly nice. You can go through the triple F (full fussy fancy) stirring procedure, managing to avoid curdling or even scrambling the egg on the way. What I've now started to do and highly recommend is to get one of the (actually delicious) ready-made packets and always have one ready in the store cupboard (most don't even need the fridge) – and there you are ! You just warm it up gently and decant into a beautiful jug. It's equally nice cooled down too, just remove any skin.

Brandy butter

Beat together *butter, sugar* and *brandy* (or other spirit – rum and cointreau are specially good).

This is the traditional accompaniment to mince pies and Christmas pudding but there's no harm in delighting people with it at other times too.

Toffee sauce

Warm equal amounts of *butter* and *soft brown sugar*, with a tablespoon of *golden syrup* till they are all melted together (about 1 minute). Serve immediately as it hardens on cooling – spectacular over ice cream.

Honey sauce

Melt some *butter*, stir in a small amount of cornflour till combined, then gradually add a good amount of clear honey, simmer for 1-2 minutes.

SPICES

There are so many – just choose your favourite(s). Ones that I specially like, and you might too, are

- Nutmeg
- Oregano
- Basil
- Cumin
- Cinnamon – I specially love this flavour and it has so many uses – great with almost everything
- Ginger – my all time favourite. Lovely either as a slight subdued touch or, as in parkin, the strong predominant flavour.

Dried bark strips, bark powder and flowers of the small tree Cinnamomum verum
By Simon A. Eugster, CC BY-SA 3.0, wiki commons

GINGER HISTORY

Unusually among spices, ginger does not grow in the wild and its actual origins are uncertain, but Indians and Chinese are believed to have produced it for over 5000 years as a tonic root to treat many ailments. The plant is now cultivated throughout the humid tropics, with India being the largest producer.

Ginger was an important export from India to the Roman Empire, where it was valued for its medicinal properties. Ginger continued to be a highly sought after commodity in Europe even after the fall of the Roman Empire, with Arab merchants controlling the trade in ginger and other spices for centuries. In the 13th and 14th centuries, the value of a pound of ginger was equivalent to the cost of a sheep. It was valued for its flavour and in medieval times was being imported in preserved form to be used in sweets. Queen Elizabeth I is said to have invented the gingerbread man, now a popular Christmas treat.

SEASONINGS

Cayenne pepper (or any form of red or chilli pepper), essential in any cook's store. A pinch or two is great for adding a touch of zzz to almost any dish, even those not normally thought of as "spicy". More if you want of course.

CAYENNE PEPPER ORIGIN

Cayenne or red pepper is a small shrub that grows up to 3 feet tall with the long thin chillies reaching around 10 cm – the hollow fruit grows into long pods that turn red, orange, or yellow when they ripen. It was first grown in Central and South America in pre-Columbian times (its name is believed to come from the native Brazilian Tupi word *'kyinha'* meaning hot pepper). Native Americans have used it as both food and medicine for at least 9,000 years. It was cultivated in Mexico 7,000 years ago and in Peru as both a food and a medicine for stomach aches, cramping pains, gas, and disorders of the circulatory system for 9,000 years.

It was brought to Europe in the fifteenth century by Christopher Columbus. From Europe, cayenne was transported to tropical and subtropical regions around the world, where it is now widely grown, especially in Africa, India and South East Asia. It is an important spice, particularly in Cajun and Creole cooking, and in the cuisines of Southeast Asia, China, Southern Italy, and Mexico. It has also been used in traditional Indian Ayurvedic, Chinese, Japanese, and Korean medicines as an oral remedy for stomach problems, poor appetite, and circulatory problems and applied to the skin for arthritis and muscle pain.

Today cayenne is used worldwide to treat a variety of health conditions, including weak digestion, chronic pain, shingles, heart disease, sore throats, headaches, high cholesterol levels, poor circulation, and toothache. For cooks it is the ultimate best spice for "hot" spicy dishes.

Salt

Seasoning with salt, and by how much, is very much a matter of opinion – it's up to your personal taste. However look out for *over*-salting (hard to correct in a hurry and unhealthy in excess); individuals can always add more at the table if they wish. So I have often not listed it in recipes, leaving it to your decision as a cook. Nevertheless salt is a famous and long-loved condiment with its own fascinating history.

THE PAST AND PRESENT OF SALT

Salt is essential for life, and saltiness is one of the basic human tastes. It is unsurprising therefore that salt is one of the oldest and most ubiquitous food seasonings, and is known to uniformly improve the taste of food, including otherwise unpalatable food. Salting, brining, and pickling are also ancient and important methods of food preservation. It is processed from salt mines, and by the evaporation of seawater (sea salt) and mineral-rich spring water in shallow pools.

Some of the earliest evidence of salt processing dates to around 6000 BC, when people living in the area of present-day Romania boiled spring water to extract salts; a salt works in China dates to approximately the same period. Salt was also prized by the ancient Hebrews, Greeks, Romans, Byzantines, Hittites, Egyptians, and Indians. Salt became an important article of trade and was transported by boat across the Mediterranean Sea, along specially built salt roads, and across the Sahara on camel caravans. The scarcity and universal need for salt have led nations to go to war over it and use it to raise tax revenues. Salt is used in religious ceremonies and has widespread cultural significance.

Pepper generally

Pepper, especially freshly ground black pepper, is a great addition to almost any savoury dish and has an even more fascinating history.

PEPPER HISTORY

Black pepper, nicknamed "black gold" and the "king of spices", is the most widely consumed spice in the world and the most important spice traded internationally.

It has been grown in India for thousands of years and was first introduced to the Europe following the 4th century BC global conquests of Alexander the Great. It was one the earliest commodities to be traded between Asia and Europe. In the Middle Ages pepper was frequently used for rent, dowry and tax. Pepper traders were numerous enough to have their own vernacular names: "Pepperer" in England, "Pfeffersacke" in Germany and "Poivrier"in France. The cities of Alexandria, Genoa and Venice carried on brisk trade in pepper in mediaeval times and they owed their prosperity to their trade in this priceless commodity.

Vasco de Gama's discovery of a sea-route to the spice lands of Malabar Coast in 1498 was triggered by his interest in spices, particularly pepper, and gave Portugal a monopoly over the spice trade. For the next two centuries, Lisbon was the richest European port precisely because it was the key trading centre for pepper and other oriental spices.

Chapter 9:
I SMELL BURNING, AND OTHER INTERESTING HAPPENINGS

If it's me or my mother you almost certainly do smell burning! And not for the first time either...

I suggest you scan through this chapter quickly now.
You won't want to be scrambling around trying to find your way
in the middle of a disaster.

First things first

Everyone has had a kitchen mishap sometime. Even the television show chefs surely have – just they don't talk about it. There are always ways round, even if at the time it feels like the end of the world. Here are some possible kitchen tragedies/mishaps, with some ideas about how to cope.

Fire and flames

- If big, call the fire brigade. Yes, *do*! And at once. That's what they're there for and they prefer sooner rather than later. Take it in your stride and welcome them with smile.
- If containable, use a fire extinguisher if you have one or smother with a generous amount of salt or baking soda or, best (since fire thrives on oxygen) a heavy floor rug or blanket.
- If someone is burnt, even slightly, swell the place with plentiful COLD WATER (under cold tap if possible), if serious call ambulance.

Burning and scorching

Burning something you're cooking – er, making it lovely and "caramelised" – is manageable but what you do depends on what it is.

Soups and casseroles

First thing, taste a spoonful from the top.

- It it tastes burnt, throw the whole thing away, leave saucepan to soak, and, easy, just substitute something else (suggestions below)
- If it tastes more or less okay you can still use some of it. Empty the unburned top part (WITHOUT SCRAPING THE BOTTOM) into a clean pan. There'll now be less than you started with so top up with, for example, a tin of soup and/or stock plus chopped vegetables (frozen peas always a brilliant, quick, standby).
- If it tastes just a smidgen scorched, disguise with some strong flavour such as cayenne pepper, ginger, curry powder, marmite, coffee, a little liqueur.
- Once reheated turn it low, so it won't happen again.

Burnt roast meat

- If scorched round the edges the inside may taste fine, just rather dry and bland (some people prefer meat well done that way), so just cut off the burnt bits and serve it, smiling, with plenty of well-seasoned gravy and perhaps a zingy sauce on the side..
- If very overdone cut into thin slices and smother with gravy or other sauce.

Other burnt main dishes

If beyond recovery, throw away and substitute something else.

Burnt bread, toast etc

This is nothing new!

- If beyond hope throw away and if possible produce an alternative.
- Otherwise simply scrape off the black into the sink and smother the surface with butter and marmalade/jam/honey/ marmite/paté. **Nice!**

Burnt cake

If burnt through, throw away (you can always make another some other day).

- If only the surface is burnt, cut off to the burnt bits, and conceal the scraped/cut places with a frilly paper or material covering.
- If it's the bottom that's burnt, turn the cake upside down, cut off the burnt layer and cover it with decorative icing.
- If the topping is burnt, scrape it off and substitute a different one (just don't let *it* burn) or cover with cream or custard.

And generally, *open the kitchen window* and, if you have one, turn on the fan extractor.

Wrong consistency

- Too runny – add oat flakes, red lentils, small pieces of partly cooked potatoes, or torn up bread, and simmer till thickened.
- Too thick – add more liquid: water, milk, stock, wine, whatever.
- Too lumpy – while still in the saucepan whisk hard by hand or, if you have one, an electric hand-held stick; or, if you have time, sieve or liquidise.
- Too salty – boil potatoes in the mixture.
- Too insipid – add seasoning, herbs, spices.
- Curdled – slowly beat in more egg yolk. Or (my system) throw away.
- Too much of the wrong flavour – add some strong counter flavour like ginger, sugar/honey, lemon juice, red pepper (don't overdo it).
- Too spicy: make sure you serve plenty of rice or similar, and put Greek yoghurt or thick sour cream on the table, it does wonders.

Oh no – out of kilter timing

It happens. All the time. How on earth did my mother-in-law get everything ready *at the same time* but when *she* came to see *me* things got ready minutes and minutes and minutes apart?

What to do? Plan beforehand. This is my sister's strategy – and *she* really *is* a good cook as well as human. She makes a list of timings (to the minute) for what has to be done when, and keeps to it. Takes a lot of stress out of things

- Always have spares or substitutes (bought or home-made) get-at-able in the background somewhere.
- Make one or, better, more courses beforehand, so they are already to hand.
- Have a place where things can keep warm while other things catch up.
- Have a good supply of drinks and nibbles so any waiting around looks part of a delightful leisure plan.
- Consider eating in stages as things get ready saying something like "you must be so hungry, don't feel you have to wait, let's start on this and then we can carry on as things get ready", or "I thought we'd try the Catalan custom of separating the meat and vegetables".

Wrong quantity

- Too much: over-catering (very common when entertaining). No problem so long as you have suitable covered containers and somewhere to store surplus food. There are some great recipes specifically for leftovers (eg colcannon, bubble and squeak).
- Too little: under catering (disaster ...). Harder – but you're sure to have something in your store cupboard or fridge you can add to the table as if it had always been planned (cheese and biscuits for example)
- Quietly supplement with a ready-stored dish or the emergency dishes listed at the end of this chapter (you'd always intended to let them try this, hadn't you ...).
- Produce extra rolls and butter or, if you have it, some of your home baked bread with the main course, or, later, a large plate of sweet biscuits, cake or chocolates with "if anyone wants to top up" or, more tactfully "I'd like to have your opinion of this, would you try a bit?"

- *Looks* make all the difference, so instead of helping things out at the table when any under supply might be visible, put it out ready on people's individual (preferably not too large) plates. It will look more.
- A rather specialised form of eventual under catering was when my parents were entertaining the local bishop and mayor with a really extravagant, for them, whole salmon laid out ready on the beautifully laid table. The guests were ushered in. There was the salmon – on the floor with the dog. After a short aghast moment everyone burst out laughing and they had a great evening. I've no idea what they ate in the end but it didn't matter.

You know – a relaxed smile or giggle can fix a multitude of things. So if you really can't conceal that there's been a bit of a disaster, tell – or make up – a hilarious story about your or your mother's worst cooking calamity. That way even if there IS still a strong smell of burning (or whatever) it'll be kept in proportion, even ADD to the story…

Generally

Don't beat yourself up, we've all been through it, cooking isn't a personality test.

Remember that guests, friends, family eating your food *don't know what your initial plan was* and the last thing they want is to feel *they* are responsible for what's going on in the kitchen. They're lucky to be sitting down to anything at all that they haven't had to worry over themselves.

Just serve it up with a smile, relax and enjoy it. You know you're a *good* bad cook really and after all who can ask for more.

This is a short chapter not because I haven't had lots of disasters (and, like my mother, more or less survived) but because you'll want somewhere to list YOUR solutions.

That way instead of turning into a screaming horror you just look up your notes and remember – "Oh yes, that's what I did … and it might make for a funny story at my next dinner party".

Good emergency dishes

* Pea and mint soup; home special soup; avocado toast; enchanted grapefruit
* Curry hurry; fry-mix special; simplest salmon
* Jamaican bananas; cream fruit; burnt orange; soufflé omelette
* Fresh fruit; cheese and biscuits; Irish coffee

These are just some examples, there are lots more – you'll build up your own list, have a store of tasty sauces, and, good-bad cook that you are, always have own emergency fall backs.

Chapter 10: THOUGHTS AND RANTS

Don't believe it

Be wary of two fetishes around just now:

- *First* that you must always, but always, cook "From Scratch". Why? What's wrong with *assembling* or arranging? After all cooking is just the process of preparing food so as to make it nourishing and attractive and appetising. And enjoyable – and what's wrong with that?
- *Second* that you must *always* buy Fresh Fresh Fresh, like from Farmers Markets and so on.

Sometimes of course it's good – and pleasant – to support local enterprise. However, nothing wrong with frozen supermarket meat and veg that is likely to be fresh and carefully selected.

Things I tell myself

There's nothing wrong about buying ready meals – so long as I then transfer them into my most beautiful crockery and avoid discussion of their origin. Don't let a guest come to "help" (hinder) you in the kitchen when you're frantically finishing up the cooking. The history of food and cooking sets things in perspective. Puts *me* in perspective.

Things my mother told me

Learn to be a time-and-motion expert – don't go three times across the room if you can get it all done in one, and for goodness sake, child, remember you have *two* hands and quite a lot of wit. Ask for help if you really need it, but mostly it's easier not. An open window and a good view to outside from the sink are worth a hundred clever recipes And whatever, hold up your head, relax and stop frowning, what's the point of being a good–bad cook if you're not enjoying it and *proud. My grandmother told me:* You're actually quite a good cook, you know. And part of history.

APPENDIX 1: THINGS

Skip this, you'll know it already – just it might be handy to keep to show a young person you might be helping to understand what it us to be a good bad cook …)

Some things worth having

Most of the dishes in this book (not quite all) use equipment and ingredients commonly in most cooks' homes, but it might be helpful to have a quick basic list (if you can't get hold of them there are often lots of just-as-good alternatives). So here are things this book has assumed you (mostly) have, besides of course some kind of a kitchen with cooker, fridge-freezer (or cold larder), sink:

Basic equipment – crockery, cutlery, kitchen knife, potato peeler, kitchen scissors (bright coloured so they don't keep disappearing), whisk (preferably electric), at least two good size saucepans and lids, frying pan, kettle, one or more oven dishes with lids, heatproof gloves, and of course a smile (*specially* the smile).

Ideally also a food processor/ liquidiser (you can manage with a sieve as we all did in the past but it takes longer and is less economical), microwave, slow cooker (brilliant), electric kettle (saves a lot of bother) and electric toaster.

NOT pretty aprons, lots of complicated fancy electrical equipment, a wine cellar, or rows of cookery books. None of these do any harm, they're quite nice in fact, even sometimes useful, but they're not needed for this guide.

A place or places to store food, with some things in it.

Store cupboard

People differ in their tastes, and available shops of course, but most of the dishes in the book (including the emergency ones) assume you'll have most or all the following so keep them replenished. They mostly come in a variety of forms – fresh, dried, frozen, or in tins or packets – any of these will generally work.

I'm prejudiced of course and have made sure to include my own favourites (you'll know by now that this is a personal, thus biased, book!). So, in alphabetical order, here's things:

- Avocadoes
- Bacon
- Baking soda
- Biscuits, sweet and plain.
- Bread (any kind, I like brown seeded and fruit loaves)
- Butter (any kind but spreadable low-fat is good)
- Cheese (any kind but strong (grated) especially useful for cooking)
- Coffee and chocolate (powdered or other)
- Cooking oil (extra virgin olive oil costly but good and goes a long way)
- Cornflour and/or custard powder
- Croutons
- Eggs
- Frozen ready meals for emergencies
- Fruit (oranges and bananas especially useful)
- Jam/marmalade
- Lemon and/or lime juice (bottled is easiest)
- Mango chutney
- Marmite
- Milk, cream, yoghurt (long-life the most convenient)

- Nuts (e g cashew, walnut, mixed) and seeds
- Oats (flaked, rolled or instant)
- One or two bottles dessert sauces
- One or two bottles wine and/or liqueur
- Onions, including some frozen (sliced)
- Other vegetables, any kind (frozen peas, broad beans and mixed Mediterranean vegetables are specially handy)
- Packets sauce, especially parsley, gravy
- Pasta
- Potatoes (both large and "new") and a selection of other root v vegetables such as carrots, parsnips, turnip/swedes, beetroot
- Rice
- Salad things like sweet pepper, tomatoes, radishes, celery
- Soy sauce
- Spices and herbs (any kind, but myself I'd go for sea-salt, black pepper, cayenne pepper, curry powder, cinnamon, ginger, rosemary, mint: nice if you can grow any herbs yourself in kitchen, window box, garden).
- Stock cubes
- Sugar (a variety, brown nicest) and/or honey/syrup
- Tins: fruit, fish (salmon, tuna and anchovy especially useful), soup, beans
- Wine vinegar

You probably have many of these and know how to use them, so – smile you good-bad cook !

APPENDIX 2: MEET THE AUTHOR

I can imagine a bit who *you* are (a good and sensible cook who perhaps, wrongly, thinks you're not up to much). But you're probably wondering who *I* am, yes?

I'm Ruth.

Not young, as you can see *... Once younger!* And happy. And with many years of experience learning to be a good-bad cook from watching my mother at her Irish open fire – and in other ways and other places too.

I suppose I would quite like to see myself as a *good* cook, bringing up, with my husband, our three very bright daughters on top of a very full-time academic post in an outstandingly pioneering university (www. ruthhfinnegan.com/ is the academic me).

The point I'm making is that, basically a teacher and researcher rather than a housewifely kind of person, for many years I did perforce manage three course dinners, mostly in time, to fill up the five of us (hence all the soups and puddings). So I *had* to discover quick, easy ways (mostly they were made from scratch too – chilled ready made meals weren't available at that time anyway, though I did definitely make use of tins and packets). I managed of course, by lots of trial and lots of error. To be honest, I ended up quite proud of myself -= a good-bad cook. And *enjoyed* it.

The rest of my experience is that I have home–cooked in four different continents (though I did fail on pumpkin pie in America): tropical and temperate, north and south; and the daughters all survived. They are now all good cooks and even, to my astonishment, say they learned some of it from me. And they all had the sense to marry truly excellent *real* good cooks.

I managed, as doubtless you do too, by shortcuts: making do; having a loving husband (more interested in his truly miraculous woodwork and his beautifully tended – by him – garden, true, than the kitchen but still helpful and *there*); admiring but on the whole (some exceptions below) not very much reading or following cookery books.

My mantra in both academic and cooking contexts became "If a thing's worth doing it's worth doing badly": I mean that it's no good chickening out, whether in writing *or* cooking, or, well, in life, just because you can't do it perfectly. If you risk it and have a go (often you haven't a choice anyway), maybe it'll turn out not so bad after all.

So you see I HAD to be a not-good cook – and still love it.

APPENDIX 3 BOOKS AND MORE

INSPIRING US

The collection I've found most inspiring is the hand–written hardback notebook started by my husband's grandmother away back then, enlarged by his wonderfully good-cook mother, with some good bits added by himself. It is precious, a link to a long long family heritage. No doubt *that* grandmother learned from *her* mother then added her own bits, and that mother from *her* grandmother, and so back and back and back through the years.

Mine is a scruffy handwritten folder of recipes and ideas in the back of my kitchen cupboard. Very personal. And, I suppose, and equally personal, this book. You might wish to do the same for your children and grandchildren - a hand-written record passed down through the family is very precious. It could be useful for yourself too – your own note book or card index with notes on your favourite easy good bad-cook dishes readily to hand.

Or perhaps you might like to collect up and publish *your* good-bad-cooking treatments with your personal advice and recipes to feed into the reservoir of human culinary culture? and to carry on the rich legacy of centuries? It is in the kitchens and oral traditions of millions of good-bad ordinary cooks all through the world that historical traditions are continually being created and recreated and passed on through the generations.

Good luck whatever, and don't hesitate, if you wish, to let me know how it's going. Maybe one day we could produce a collaborative supplement between us – after all there's no end to good-bad cooking.

Books

Here are some of my favourite food and cookery books. I like them for many reasons, not just, as you'll see, for their recipes and advice.

- **Ministry of Agriculture and Fisheries [UK]**, Domestic preservation of fruit and vegetables, 1948. I really warm to this because it was such a surprise to find that, yes, cooking is a way of "preserving" fruit and vegetables (as in jam); also because it was given to us by a very beloved gentle uncle on the only occasion he came to stay: he was a ship's engineer and a fine cook.
- **Bee Nilson,** The Penguin cookery book, 1952. A really sensible clear handbook with a New Zealand background (but useful anywhere); my daughters fought over which of them would get my battered old copy - I kept it!
- **Princess Gardens School Belfast,** Chefs galore, 1965. I like this book both because of its mix of traditional recipes with the wild and wonderful and because it must have been one of the earliest of the charity cookbooks. I was given it by a close friend of my mother's who was, I think, personally involved in its creation.
- **Madeleine Bingham,** Something's burning - the bad cook's guide, 1968. Brilliant, clearly one of my inspirations and supports.
- Susan Parkinson and Peggy Stacey, A taste of the tropics, 1972. This wonderfully comprehensive, well organised, and hugely informative book was a constant companion during the three years we spent in Fiji.
- **Beryl Downing,** Quick cook, recipes in under 30 minutes, 1981. It really does work!
- **Maria Luisa and Jack Denton Scott and others,** The incredible potato c cookbook, 1992. This absolutely lives up to its title and reminded me of so many potato dishes I thought I'd forgotten.
- **John Edwards** (translator) The Roman cookery of Apicius, 2009. I like this both because, with its date in the first century AD, it's the oldest cookbook we have (though there must have been others before that too), and because of

its range of varied and surprising recipes from purely natural ingredients.

- **Katharine Whitehorn**, Cooking in a bed sitter, 2003. Really sensible, lots of constructive suggestions I'd never thought of that would be useful anywhere.
- **Louise Bennett Weaver**, A thousand ways to please a husband, 2012. Reprint of an early 20th century book complete with (often very amusing) period dialogue appropriate to the time. Practical and down to earth, uncomplicated and without exotic ingredients or "advanced" techniques. I specially like it for the silly reason that when I sent a copy of it to a friend in South Africa the customs officials held it up for months, thinking, we presume, that it should be banned as .... well, you can imagine! When they did get to look at it properly they must have been very disappointed! So it finally got delivered.
- **Brian McDermott**, Donegal table: delicious everyday cooking, 2018. Well, with y Donegal background I would like this one wouldn't I - but I think anyone would: tasty, healthy food from traditional recipes and local produce that every family could make and enjoy.

Other publications I've found helpful for their information or approach are:
- **Claude Levi-Strauss**, The raw and the cooked, 1969.
- **Mary Douglas**, "Deciphering a meal", in Implicit meanings, select essays in anthropology, 1975.
- **Libby Purves**, How not to be a perfect mother, 2004.
- **Maguelonne Toussaint-Samat**, A history of food, 2008.
- **Tom Standage**, An edible history of humanity, 2009.
- **Pete Brown**, The apple orchard: the story of our most English fruit, 2017.
- **Alphonse de Candolle**, Origin of cultivated plants, 2020 (English translation of the 1886 edition).
- **David Campbell Callender**, Grass, miracle from the earth, 2020.
- **Alan Barnard**, Hunters and gatherers, 2020.

- Paula Erizanu "From birch-tree juice to Christmas bread, our food tells the story of who we are", The Guardian, 25 December 2023.
- **Johan Pottier**, Anthropology of food, the social dynamics of food security, 1999.
- Also that amazing source, *Wikipedia*

And thank you to those unnamed friends from many lands who have allowed me to add their dishes and their experience here.

www.ruthhfinnegan.com

Chapter Contents

Here is some space to add your own notes: for example,
ingredients, quantities, timings, result!

_____

_____

_____

_____

_____

_____

_____

_____

_____

_____

Milton Keynes UK
Ingram Content Group UK Ltd.
UKHW050158100524
442457UK00005B/28